Fodor's InFocus

CAYMAN ISLANDS

Excerpted from *Fodor's Essential Caribbean*   JUL - - 2018

14

TOP EXPERIENCES

The Cayman Islands offer terrific experiences that should be on every traveler's list. Here are Fodor's top picks for a memorable trip.

1 Seven Mile Beach

Those who love long, broad, uninterrupted sweeps of champagne-hued sand will be thrilled with Grand Cayman's longest beach. *(Ch. 6)*

2 Bird-watching on the Sister Islands

The Booby Pond on Little Cayman and the Brac's Parrot Reserve are just two of the gorgeous areas set aside for communing with nature. *(Ch. 7 & 8)*

3 Buying Crafts, Cayman Brac

Some of the best local craftspeople, including Annalee Ebanks (thatch-weaving) and Tenson Scott (caymanite carving), are found on the Brac. *(Ch. 7)*

4 George Town, Grand Cayman

In addition to dynamite duty-free shopping, the handsome waterfront capital hosts the historic Cayman Islands National Museum. *(Ch. 2)*

5 Pirates Point, Little Cayman

The dinners here aren't quite as elegant or complex as what you might find at one of Grand Cayman's top spots, but the bon mots and bonhomie are unmatched. *(Ch. 8)*

6 Queen Elizabeth II Botanic Garden

Critically endangered blue iguanas have found a home at this park, where you learn about their life cycles, then stroll the peaceful, gorgeously laid-out gardens. *(Ch. 2)*

7 Stingray City, Grand Cayman

You can interact with gracefully balletic, silken stingrays, so "tame" you can feed them as they beg for handouts on this shallow sandbar in the North Sound. *(Ch. 6)*

8 Diving Bloody Bay Wall

One of the top dive sites in the world plunges from 18 feet to more than a mile into the Cayman Trench; the visibility is remarkable. *(Ch. 6)*

9 Barefoot Man at the Reef Resort

Head to Pelican's Reef on the East End of Grand Cayman to hear the blond Calypsonian, Barefoot Man (née George Nowak), a beloved island icon. *(Ch. 5)*

10 Happy Hour, Grand Cayman

Such popular waterfront spots as Rackam's and The Wharf serve creative cocktails and reel in the revelers for sunset tarpon feeding. *(Ch. 5)*

11 Owen Island, off Little Cayman

Easily accessible by kayak from Little Cayman's "mainland," Owen Island appeals to snorkelers and romantics, who have their choice of captivating coves. *(Ch. 8)*

12 Local Food, Grand Cayman

Sample mouth- and eye-watering jerk chicken from a roadside stall or George Town shack. A few local chefs even serve meals in their homes. *(Ch. 3)*

13 Blue by Eric Ripert, at the Ritz-Carlton

The wine-pairing menu at Le Bernardin chef Eric Ripert's only Caribbean restaurant is the kind of epicurean experience that comes along once in a blue moon. *(Ch. 3)*

14 Underwater Sculpture, Cayman Brac

Nature's artistry is matched by the world's largest (and still growing) underwater installation, the sculptor Foots's gorgeously imagined, impressively engineered Lost City of Atlantis. *(Ch. 7)*

CONTENTS

ABOUT THIS GUIDE

Fodor's Recommendations

Everything in this guide is worth doing—we don't cover what isn't—but exceptional sights, hotels, and restaurants are recognized with additional accolades. Fodor'sChoice ★ indicates our top recommendations. Care to nominate a new place? Visit Fodors.com/contact-us.

Trip Costs

We list prices wherever possible to help you budget well. Hotel and restaurant price categories from $ to $$$$ are noted alongside each recommendation. For hotels, we include the lowest cost of a standard double room in high season. For restaurants, we cite the average price of a main course at dinner or, if dinner isn't served, at lunch. For attractions, we always list adult admission fees; discounts are usually available for children, students, and senior citizens.

Hotels

Our local writers vet every hotel to recommend the best overnights in each price category, from budget to expensive. Unless otherwise specified, you can expect private bath, phone, and TV in your room. For expanded hotel reviews visit Fodors.com.

Restaurants

Unless we state otherwise, restaurants are open for lunch and dinner daily. We mention dress code only when there's a specific requirement and reservations only when they're essential or not accepted.

Credit Cards

The hotels and restaurants in this guide typically accept credit cards. If not, we'll say so.

Top Picks

★ Fodor'sChoice

Listings

⊠ Address
⊠ Branch address
⌖ Mailing address
☎ Telephone
🖷 Fax
⊕ Website
✉ E-mail

🎫 Admission fee
☉ Open/closed times
Ⓜ Subway
⊹ Directions or Map coordinates

Hotels & Restaurants

🏨 Hotel
↩ Number of rooms
🍽 Meal plans

✕ Restaurant
☟ Reservations
🛗 Dress code
▭ No credit cards
$ Price

Other

⇨ See also
☞ Take note
🏌 Golf facilities

EXPERIENCE THE CAYMAN ISLANDS

WHAT'S WHERE

Caribbean Sea

DISTANCE ON MAP IS COMPRESSED

LITTLE CAYMAN

Jacksons Pt.
Bloody Bay Marine Park Gov.
Anchorage Gore Bird
Bay **South** Sanctuary
Town South Hole
West End Point Sound

Edward Bodden Airfield

Head of Barkers

Hell

MARINE PARK
Rum Point

Seven Mile Beach

WEST BAY A1

Water Cay Old Man Bay A3

West Bay Cayman Kai Malportas OLD
HUTLAND Pond MAN
Booby BAY
Cay

Owen Roberts International Airport *North Sound* **GRAND CAYMAN**

George Town PEASE A4 HALF
BAY BREAKERS MOON
NORTH BAY
SOUND A3
ESTATES BELFORD A3 Pease A3
NEWLANDS ESTATES Bay Ironshore
SAVANNAH A2 **Bodden Town** Point

A5 Bodden
Southweat Bay
Point

1 **Grand Cayman.** The Cayman Islands' main island offers the longest, liveliest sandy strand (Seven Mile Beach), great diving, fine dining, upscale resorts, surprisingly varied nightlife, and an attractive waterfront capital with duty-free shopping in George Town. Despite the development and congestion around Seven Mile Beach and George Town, the neighborhoods

of West Bay and East End are mellow and filled with natural wonders.

2 **Cayman Brac.** The archipelago's most rugged, dramatically scenic island is known for its bullying bluff, which vaults 140 feet. The bird-watching, caving, hiking, and rock climbing (experienced only with your own gear) are phenomenal, and the island is just as spectacular

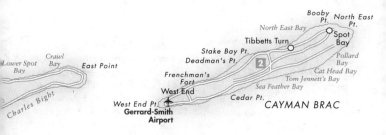

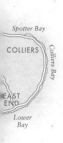

Caribbean

underwater for divers and snorkelers. The Brac is laid-back, friendly, and cheap, with affordable villas to rent and small inns and resorts.

3 Little Cayman. The smallest of the Cayman Islands is the least developed, most unspoiled in the chain. Ecotourists can get back to nature (but not the basics) at splendid little resorts catering to divers and birders. You'll find world-famous dive sites like Bloody Bay Marine Park, equally fantastic fishing (especially light-tackle), secluded beaches, and fabulous bird-watching along the shore and wetlands covering nearly half the island.

CAYMAN ISLANDS PLANNER

Island Activities

Diving is a major draw; the Bloody Bay Wall off the coast of Little Cayman is one of the Caribbean's top dive destinations. There are many other great shore diving sites convenient to Grand Cayman.

On Grand Cayman, a dive or snorkeling trip to **Stingray City** is very popular. There's good off-the-beach snorkeling in West Bay Cemetery, at Rum Point, and at Smith's Cove in Grand Cayman.

On land, Grand Cayman has the most to offer, with plenty of tours and activities, including **semisubmersible tours** of the bay.

Grand Cayman's **Seven Mile Beach** is one of the Caribbean's finest long stretches of sand. Little Cayman has the best beaches of the Sister Islands, especially Owen Island and Point of Sand.

Rock climbers have now discovered the Brac's limestone bluff.

Logistics

Getting to the Islands: There are plenty of nonstop flights to Grand Cayman (GCM) from the United States; from there you can hop over to the Brac (CYB) and Little Cayman (LYB) on a small plane.

Hassle Factor: Low for Grand Cayman; medium to high for Little Cayman and Cayman Brac.

Nonstops: You can fly nonstop to Grand Cayman from Atlanta (Delta, three times weekly), Boston (US Airways and JetBlue once weekly), Charlotte (US Airways), Detroit (Delta once weekly), Fort Lauderdale (Cayman Airways), Houston (United once weekly), Miami (American, Cayman Airways), Minneapolis (Delta once weekly), New York–JFK (Cayman Airways daily, JetBlue three times weekly, Delta once weekly), New York–Newark (United once weekly), Philadelphia (US Airways once weekly), and Tampa (Cayman Airways).

On the Ground: In Grand Cayman you must take a taxi or rent a car at the airport, since most hotels are not permitted to offer airport shuttles. Hotel pickup is more readily available on Cayman Brac and Little Cayman.

Renting a Car: It's possible to get by without a car on Grand Cayman if you are staying in the Seven Mile Beach area. If you want to explore the rest of the island—or if you are staying elsewhere—you'll need a car. Though less necessary on Cayman Brac or Little Cayman, cars are available on both islands. Driving is on the left, and you need a local driving permit, available at the car-rental office for $20.

Where to Stay

Grand Cayman: Grand Cayman has plenty of medium-size resorts as well as the Ritz-Carlton, the Westin, and Kimpton Seafire—large, comparatively high-rise resorts—on Seven Mile Beach. The island also has a wide range of condos and villas, many in resort-like compounds on or near Seven Mile Beach and the Cayman Kai area. There are even a few small guesthouses for budget-minded visitors.

The Sister Islands: Cayman Brac has mostly intimate resorts, condos, and villas. Little Cayman has a mix of small resorts and villas, most appealing to divers.

Hotel and Restaurant Costs

Prices in the restaurant reviews are the average cost of a main course at dinner or, if dinner is not served, at lunch; taxes and service charges are generally included. Prices in the hotel reviews are the lowest cost of a standard double room in high season, excluding taxes, service charges, and meal plans (except at all-inclusives). Prices for rentals are the lowest per-night cost for a one-bedroom unit in high season.

Tips for Travelers

All visitors must have a valid passport and a return or ongoing ticket to enter the Cayman Islands.

The minimum legal drinking age in the Cayman Islands is 18.

Electricity is reliable and is the same as in the United States (110 volts/60 cycles). U.S. electrical appliances will work just as if at home.

You should not need to change money in Grand Cayman, because U.S. dollars are readily accepted. ATMs generally offer the option of U.S. or Cayman dollars. The Cayman dollar is pegged to the U.S. dollar at the rate of approximately $1.25 to CI$1. Be sure you know which currency is being quoted when making a purchase.

IF YOU LIKE

Getting Away from It All

Though Grand Cayman's Seven Mile Beach is completely developed, other areas of the island still offer respite from the crowds, as do the Sister Islands. Here are some ideas for romantic R&R:

Pirates Point and The Southern Cross Club, Little Cayman. You can't go wrong with either of Little Cayman's upscale yet down-home intimate beachfront resorts.

Lighthouse Point, Grand Cayman. This ecocentric hideaway recycles practically everything, allowing guests to get back to nature but not the basics.

Cayman Breakers, Cayman Brac. Tucked away at the remotest point on the Brac, this condo complex satisfies any desire for seclusion; the owners have built an even more elegant complex next door.

The Wyndham Reef, Grand Cayman. If you crave activity and facilities galore, yet still value privacy, this midsize resort fits the bill on Grand Cayman's East End.

Great Eating

Foodies can savor a smorgasbord of gastronomic goodies, from sophisticated fusion fare to fiery local cuisine and everything in between. Try these special spots:

Bàcaro, Grand Cayman. Imagine a Caribbean version of Venice, and savor delectable *cicchetti* (tapas-style nibbles) at this handsome new eatery.

Blue by Eric Ripert, Grand Cayman. Ripert's NYC seafood-centric eatery, Le Bernardin, goes coastal with shipshape results.

Mizu, Grand Cayman. This popular pan-Asian eatery is full of well-prepared and mouthwatering temptations.

Morgan's Harbour, Grand Cayman. Enjoy the stellar views of fishing dinghies and pleasure craft cruising the North Sound alongside pub grub elevated to an art form.

Cimboco, Grand Cayman. Everything about this spot is creative, from the boldly colored decor to the innovative takes on Caribbean cuisine.

Pirate's Point, Little Cayman. It's practically worth a day trip from Grand Cayman to enjoy the food and conversation at this lovely retreat.

The Water

Bloody Bay and Stingray City are the showcase attractions in Cayman, but here are some suggestions for other stellar sites and aquatic activities:

Wreck Diving, Grand Cayman, and Cayman Brac. The Cayman Islands government sank the decommissioned 251-foot USS *Kittiwake* to create another artificial reef, while the Brac counters with the 330-foot *Capt. Keith Tibbetts*, a virtual fireworks display of reef life.

Shore Diving, Grand Cayman. Silverside minnows swarm in the grottoes at Eden Rock, forming liquid silver-lamé curtains of fish; its neighbor, the Devil's Grotto, resembles an abstract marine painting.

Kayaking, Grand Cayman. Glide through protected mangrove wetlands teeming with a unique ecosystem; the Bio Bay tour on moonless nights is unforgettable.

Sportfishing, Cayman Brac, and Little Cayman. Both Sister Islands offer sensational bonefishing in the flats, as well as deep-sea fishing for marlin, wahoo, and sushi-grade tuna.

Shopping

Bring home mementos from these local shops:

Caymanian Crafts, Grand Cayman, and Cayman Brac. The Cayman Craft Market and fun funky stores like Pure Art sell everything from local preserves to paintings, while Tenson Scott on the Brac is famed for his Caymanite creations.

Rum and More Rum, Grand Cayman. Cayman's own Seven Fathoms Rum produces a mellow spirit via a unique underwater aging process, while Tortuga Rum is celebrated for its rum-soaked cakes in many flavors.

Art, Grand Cayman. Find original paintings and sculptures by Cayman artists, including Al Ebanks, Luelan Bodden, Gordon Solomon, Nickola McCoy-Snell, and Randy and Nasaria Suckoo Cholette.

Jewelry, Grand Cayman. Downtown George Town is practically one giant duty-free shopping center, highlighting numerous name brands and individual jewelers, while conspicuous consumption continues in the malls along Seven Mile Beach.

WHEN TO GO

The high season in the Cayman Islands is traditionally winter—from December 15 to April 15—when northern weather is at its worst. As it's the most popular time to visit, most resorts are heavily booked. You must make reservations at least two or three months in advance for top-rated places (sometimes a year in advance for the most exclusive spots). Hotel prices drop 20%–50% after April 15; airfares and cruise prices also fall. Saving money isn't the only reason to visit the Cayman Islands during the off-season: in summer, the sea is calmer (ideal for diving—except when tropical storms roil the waters), and things move at a slower pace. The water is clearer for snorkeling and smoother for sailing in May, June, and July, when the big game fish, though abundant year-round, really run riot.

Climate

The average daily temperature is about 80°F, and there isn't much variation from the coolest to the warmest months (the same applies to the water temperature). Rainfall averages 50 to 60 inches per year (less in the more arid Sister Islands and Grand Cayman's East End). But in the tropics, rainstorms tend to be sudden and brief, often erupting early in the morning and at dusk. Toward the end of summer, hurricane season begins in earnest. Starting in June, islanders pay close attention to the tropical waves as they form and travel across the Atlantic from Africa. In an odd paradox, tropical storms passing by leave behind the sunniest and clearest days you'll ever see.

Festivals and Events

In January, attend the celebrity-heavy **Cayman Cookout**, co-organized by top toque Eric Ripert, followed by Taste of Cayman in February. February also celebrates Cayman culture with the **Arts Festival.** The island explodes with color every April with its take on Carnival called **Batabano.** May's **Cayman Islands International Fishing Tournament** lures anglers from around the world. November's **GimiSTORY** celebrates the region's rich oral storytelling tradition. The blockbuster event, though, is November's **Pirates Week Festival,** when Grand Cayman turns into one giant 11-day party, featuring parades, costume competitions, street dances, Heritage Days, mock pirate invasions, sporting events, fireworks, and delicious local grub.

1

GREAT ITINERARIES

It's a shame that so few visitors (other than divers) spend time on more than one island in a single trip. If you have more than a week, you can certainly spend some quality time on both Grand Cayman and one of its Sister Islands.

If You Have 3 Days

Ensconce yourself at a resort along Grand Cayman's **Seven Mile Beach**, spending your first day luxuriating on the sand. On Day 2, get your feet wet at **Stingray City and Sandbar** in West Bay, where you can feed the alien-looking gliders by hand. Splurge for a great dinner on your second night at **Blue by Eric Ripert**. On your last day, head into **George Town** for some shopping. Have lunch with scintillating harbor views at **Lobster Pot** or **Casanova** before soaking up some last rays of sun.

If You Have 7 Days

Because divers need to decompress before their return flight, the last day should be spent sightseeing on Grand Cayman. **The Cayman Turtle Farm** is an expensive but exceptional marine theme park, and well worth a visit. On the East End, hike the pristine **Mastic Trail**, then stroll through the gorgeous grounds at **Queen Elizabeth II Botanic Park.** Spend your final morning in George Town, perhaps snorkeling **Eden Rock.** If you need a break

from Seven Mile Beach, spend a full day beachcombing at the savagely beautiful **Barkers** in West Bay. If you have a car, explore the East End natural attractions, and grab lunch at the **Lighthouse.** Head east another day to visit historic **Pedro St. James Castle**; drive through the original capital, **Bodden Town,** then spend the afternoon (lunch, swimming, and water sports) at **Cayman Kai/Rum Point.**

If You Have 10 Days

With 10 days, you can spend time on two or even all three islands. Begin on Cayman Brac; after diving the **north coast** walls, **MV Capt. Keith Tibbetts**, and the **Lost City of Atlantis** (or just lying on the beach), save a morning to hike through the **Parrot Reserve** out to the **East End Lighthouse** for sensational views. You can also climb the Lighthouse Steps which lead to **Peter's Cave.** On Little Cayman, chill out picnicking on **Owen Island,** and don't miss the **Booby Pond Nature Reserve.** Spend at least two nights on Grand Cayman.

WEDDINGS AND HONEYMOONS

The Cayman Islands, especially Grand Cayman, are one of the Caribbean's foremost honeymoon destinations. Destination weddings are also particularly popular on Grand Cayman, where the larger resorts have wedding planners to help you with the paperwork and details.

The Big Day

Choosing the Location. Choose from beaches, bluffs, gardens, private residences, historic buildings, resort lawns, and places of worship for the ceremony or reception. Most couples choose to say their vows on Seven Mile Beach. Underwater weddings in full scuba gear with schools of fish as impromptu witnesses are also possible (kissing with mask on optional); Cathy Church can photograph the undersea event (⇨ *Shopping in Chapter 2*). You can also get hitched while hovering in a helicopter. If you decide to hold the event outdoors, be sure you have a backup plan in case of rain.

Finding a Wedding Planner. If you're planning to invite more than an officiant and your loved one to the ceremony, consider an on-island wedding planner (larger resorts have on-site wedding planners who can provide you with a detailed list of their services, or you can hire an independent planner), who can help with the location, floral scheme, finding a photographer, and planning the menu. They'll also suggest local traditions to incorporate into your ceremony.

Legal Requirements. Documentation can be prepared ahead of time or in one day while on the island. A minimal residency waiting period, blood test, and shots are not required.

You need to supply a Cayman Islands international embarkation/disembarkation card, as well as proof of identity (a passport or certified copy of your birth certificate signed by a notary public), and age (those under 18 must provide parental consent). If you've been married before, you must provide proof of divorce with the original or certified copy of the divorce decree if applicable, or a copy of the death certificate if your previous spouse died. You must list a marriage officer on the application, and you need at least two witnesses; if you haven't come with friends or family, the marriage officer can help you with that, too. A marriage license costs CI$200 (US$250).

Photographs. Deciding whether to use the photographer supplied by your resort or an independent photographer is an important choice. Resorts that host a lot of weddings usually have their own photographers, but you can also find independent, professional island-based photographers, and an independent wedding planner will know the best in the area.

The Honeymoon

If you choose to honeymoon at a resort, you can spend it getting champagne and strawberries delivered to your room each morning, floating in a swimming pool each afternoon, and dining in a five-star restaurant at night. Grand Cayman offers resort options in different price ranges. Whether you want a luxurious experience or a more modest one, you'll certainly find someplace romantic to which you can escape. For a more secluded stay, opt for a private vacation-rental home or condo.

KIDS AND FAMILIES

Grand Cayman and, to a much lesser extent, Cayman Brac jump with activities and attractions that will keep children of all ages (and their parents) happily occupied. Some resorts and hotels welcome children, others do not, and still others restrict kids to off-season visits. All but the fanciest (and most expensive) restaurants are kid-friendly.

Family-Friendly Resorts

The **Ritz-Carlton**, the biggest and most fashionable of the island's resorts, welcomes children at any time with "edu-tainment" programs for all ages, including Jean-Michel Cousteau's Ambassadors of the Environment initiative introducing Cayman's culture and ecology. Less pricey is **Grand Cayman Marriott Beach Resort** on Seven Mile Beach which has children's programs. Many of the condo complexes toward the northern end of Seven Mile Beach, such as **Christopher Columbus** and **Discovery Point Club**, offer good value and a wide rock-free strand. On Cayman Brac, the **Brac Reef Beach Resort** is best equipped for families. Little Cayman is too quiet for most kids, but the **Little Cayman Beach Resort** can keep children occupied while their parents dive.

Family-Friendly Dining and Activities

Dining out with the family is not an issue, as Grand Cayman has more restaurants than you can count serving a virtual United Nations of cuisines. The Sister Islands are much more limited in their offerings, though the friendly locals will do their utmost to please finicky palates. **Camana Bay** is definitely family-friendly, from climbing the Observation Tower to see gorgeous panoramas, to splashing in the fountains and watching the frequent street performers. Most of the islands' water-based activities cater to kids, including the **Atlantis semisubmersible, Stingray City snorkeling tours,** and the **Dolphin Discovery.** The attractions at the **Cayman Turtle Centre,** including the predator reef and breeding facility, mesmerize all ages, as will learning about blue iguanas at their habitat in the **Queen Elizabeth II Botanical Garden.** Pipes, ramps, and rails galore, not to mention a wave-surf machine at **Black Pearl Skate & Surf Park** appeal to both kids and adults.

EXPLORING GRAND CAYMAN

With Shopping

Updated
by Jordan
Simon

THOUGH GRAND CAYMAN IS MOST celebrated for its aquatic activities, there's no shortage of diversions to please landlubbers, history buffs, the ecocentric, and families, from a turtle farm to ruined fortifications. It's just as alluring on land as underwater. Though not lush, the surrounding scenery can seamlessly shift from arid semi-desert to tropical hardwood forests that pierce the sky like cathedral spires. Many attractions admirably attempt to foster greater understanding of the environment and the importance of responsible stewardship of our resources.

Window-shopping in the capital, George Town, ranks as many visitors' favorite form of recreation and sightseeing. Not only will you find no additional sales tax, but there's duty-free merchandise aplenty. And though most people's image of Grand Cayman is bustling Seven Mile Beach, there are rural, pastoral pockets where if time doesn't stand still, it slows to a turtle's steady crawl. This is where travelers can experience the "real" Cayman, including craft traditions such as thatch weaving that have nearly vanished.

EXPLORING GRAND CAYMAN

The historic capital of George Town, on the southeast corner of Grand Cayman, is easy to explore on foot. If you're a shopper, you can spend days here; otherwise, an hour will suffice for a tour of the downtown area. To see the rest of the island, rent a car or scooter or take a guided tour. The portion of the island called West Bay is noted for its jumble of neighborhoods, many featuring ornate Edwardian homes built by seafarers, nautical tour companies (and real fishing fleet) at Morgan's Harbour, and a few attractions. When traffic is heavy, it's about a half hour to West Bay from George Town, even with the newer bypass road that runs parallel to West Bay Road. The less-developed North Side and East End have natural attractions from blowholes to botanical gardens, as well as the remains of the island's original settlements. Plan on at least 45 minutes for the drive out from George Town (more than an hour during rush hours). You need a day to explore the entire island—including a stop at a beach for a picnic or swim.

CRUISE CRUSH. **On certain days George Town, Seven Mile Beach, and even West Bay's attractions crawl with cruise-ship hordes.**

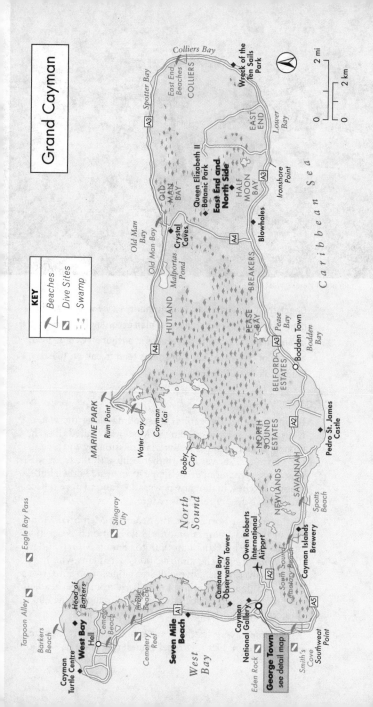

Grand Cayman

KEY

Beaches
Dive Sites
Swamp

Eagle Ray Pass

Tarpoon Alley

Barkers Beach

Head of Barkers

Cayman Turtle Centre

West Bay
Hell

Cemetery Beach

Cemetery Reef

Seven Mile Beach

West Bay

Eden Rock

Cayman National Gallery

George Town see detail map

Smith's Cove

Southweat Point

Owen Roberts International Airport

Camana Bay Observation Tower

Public Beach

A1

Stingray City

North Sound

Marine Park

Rum Point

Water Cay

Cayman Kai

Booby Cay

North Sound Estates

Newlands

Savannah

Spotts Beach

Cayman Islands Brewery

South Sound

Smith Barcadere

A2

A5

Pedro St. James Castle

Belford Estates

Bodden Town

Pease Bay

Bodden Bay

A3

Breakers

Blowholes

A4

Malportas Pond

Hutland

Old Man Bay

Old Man Bay

Crystal Caves

Old Man Bay

Queen Elizabeth II Botanic Park

East End and North Side

Half Moon Bay

Ironshore Point

Lower Bay

East End

A3

Spotter Bay

A3

East End Beaches

Colliers

Colliers Bay

Wreck of the Ten Sails Park

Caribbean Sea

0   2 km

0   2 mi

An aerial view of West Bay

Check the Cayman Island Port Authority (⊕ www.caymanport. com) for the latest schedule, and plan accordingly. There may be anywhere from one to three ships at anchor off George Town any day of the week, but more ships tend to call on Tuesday, Wednesday, and Thursday.

GEORGE TOWN

Begin exploring the capital by strolling along the water-front, Harbour Drive, to **Elmslie Memorial United Church,** named after the first Presbyterian missionary to serve in the Caymans. Its vaulted timber ceiling (built from sal-vaged wreck material in the shape of an upside-down hull), wooden arches, mahogany pews, and tranquil nave reflect the island's deeply religious nature.

Just north near Fort Street, the **Seamen's Memorial Monument** lists 153 names on an old navigational beacon; a bronze piece by Canadian sculptor Simon Morris, titled *Tradition,* honors the almost 500 Caymanians who have lost their lives at sea. Dive-industry pioneer Bob Soto, wife Suzy, and daughter-in-law Leslie Bergstrom spearheaded the project, which Prince Edward unveiled during the 2003 quincentennial celebrations.

A few steps away lie the scant remains of **Fort George,** constructed in 1790 to repel plundering pirates; it also

BEST BETS

■ **Feeling Blue.** Visit the endangered blue iguana compound at the glorious Queen Elizabeth II Botanic Park.

■ **Petting a Turtle.** Though it's pricey, the Turtle Centre encapsulates everything that makes Cayman special. Admission to its world-class turtle research center/farm includes other star residents, from cockatoos to sharks.

■ **Reliving History.** Pedro St. James Castle bears eloquent testimony to Caymanian struggles for democracy, freedom, and survival against the elements.

■ **National Trust–worthy.** The National Trust is an admirable institution dedicated to preserving the Caymanian environment and culture. If you're on the island when they're running a tour (such as to the bat caves or historic homes) or a demonstration (cooking, thatch weaving), make sure to attend.

■ **Local Legend Guy Harvey.** When he's not off adventuring, acclaimed marine biologist-artist Guy Harvey is usually in his amazing gallery-shop; buy a print, ask him to sign it, and converse on conservation.

functioned as a watch post during World War II to scan for German subs.

In front of the court building, in the center of town, names of influential Caymanians are inscribed on the **Wall of History,** which also commemorates the islands' quincentennial. Across the street is the Cayman Islands **Legislative Assembly Building,** next door to the **1919 Peace Memorial Building.** A block south is the horseshoe-shape **General Post Office,** built in 1939 at the tail end of the art deco period. Let the kids pet the big blue iguana statues.

★ Fodor's Choice **Cayman Islands National Museum.** Built in 1833,
FAMILY the historically significant clapboard home of the national museum has had several different incarnations over the years, serving as courthouse, jail, post office, and dance hall. It features an ongoing archaeological excavation of the Old Gaol and excellent 3-D bathymetric displays, murals, dioramas, and videos that illustrate local geology, flora and fauna, and island history. The first floor focuses on natural history, including a microcosm of Cayman ecosystems, from beaches to dry woodlands and swamps, and offers such interactive elements as a simulated sub. Upstairs, the cultural exhibit features renovated murals, video history

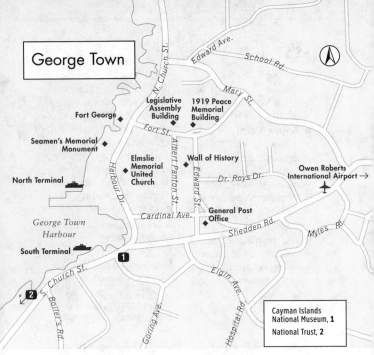

George Town

Fort George
Seamen's Memorial Monument
North Terminal
George Town Harbour
South Terminal

Legislative Assembly Building
1919 Peace Memorial Building
Elmslie Memorial United Church
Wall of History
General Post Office
Owen Roberts International Airport →

N. Church St.
Edward Ave.
School Rd.
Mary St.
Fort St.
Harbour Dr.
Albert Panton St.
Edward St.
Dr. Roys Dr.
Cardinal Ave.
Shedden Rd.
Myles Rd.
Elgin Ave.
S. Church St.
Boiler's Rd.
Goring Ave.
Hospital Rd.

1

2

Cayman Islands National Museum, **1**
National Trust, **2**

reenactments, and 3-D back panels in display cases holding thousands of artifacts ranging from a 14-foot catboat with animatronic captain to old coins and rare documents. These paint a portrait of daily life and past industries, such as shipbuilding and turtling, and stress Caymanians' resilience when they had little contact with the outside world. There are also temporary exhibits focusing on aspects of Caymanian culture, a local art collection, and interactive displays for kids. ⊠ *Harbour Dr., George Town* ☎ *345/949–8368* ⊕ *www.museum.ky* ⊒ *$8.*

NEED A BREAK? **Full of Beans Cafe.** On the surprisingly large, eclectic, Asian-tinged menu using ultrafresh ingredients, standouts include homemade carrot cake, mango smoothies, cranberry-Brie-pecan salad, and rosemary-roasted portobello and pesto chicken panini. The espresso martini will perk up anyone wanting a pick-me-up. Owner Cindy Butler fashions a feast for weary eyes as well, with rotating artworks (many for sale) and stylish mosaic mirrors contrasting with faux-brick walls and vintage hardwood tables. ⊠ Pasadora Pl., Smith Rd., George Town ☎ 345/943–2326, 345/814–0157 ⊕ www.fullofbeans.ky.

Maritime Heritage Trail

CLOSE UP

The National Trust for the Cayman Islands, National Museum, National Archive, Sister Islands Nature Tourism Project, and Department of the Environment have collaborated on a series of land-based sightseeing trails on Grand Cayman and the Sister Islands that commemorate the country's maritime heritage. Shoreside signs around the islands denote points of access and explain their historic or natural significance, from shipwreck sites to shore-

bird-sighting spots, chandlers' warehouses to lighthouses.

Brochures and posters are available at the National Trust and tourism offices on each island, as well as at many hotels. They provide additional information on turtling, shipbuilding, salvaging, fishing, and other sea-based economies. The project provides visitors with interactive and educational entertainment as they explore the islands.

★ **Fodor's Choice National Trust.** This office provides a map of historic and natural attractions, books and guides to Cayman, and information on its website about everything from iguanas to schoolhouses. The expanded gift shop provides one-stop souvenir shopping, from hair clips to logwood carvings to coconut soaps, all made on the island. Regularly scheduled activities range from boat tours through the forests of the Central Mangrove Wetlands, to cooking classes with local chefs, to morning walking tours of historic George Town. The office is walkable from George Town, but be aware that it's a 20-minute hike from downtown, often in the heat. ⊠ *Dart Park, 558 S. Church St., George Town* 🕾 *345/749–1121* ⊕ *www.nationaltrust.org.ky.*

SEVEN MILE BEACH

FAMILY **Camana Bay Observation Tower.** This 75-foot structure provides striking 360-degree panoramas of otherwise flat Grand Cayman, sweeping from George Town and Seven Mile Beach to the North Sound. The double-helix staircase is impressive in its own right. Running alongside the steps (an elevator is also available), a floor-to-ceiling mosaic replicates the look and feel of a dive from seabed to surface. Constructed of tiles in 114 different colors, it's one of the world's largest marine-themed mosaics. Benches and lookout points let you take in the views as you ascend. Afterward you can enjoy 500-acre Camana Bay's gar-

A traditional Cayman cottage at Boatswain's Beach

dens, waterfront boardwalk, and pedestrian paths lined with shops and restaurants, or frequent live entertainment. ⊠ *Between Seven Mile Beach and North Sound, 2 miles (3 km) north of George Town, Camana Bay* ☎ *345/640–3500* ⊕ *www.camanabay.com* ⊠ *Free.*

★ Fodor'sChoice **National Gallery.** A worthy nonprofit, this museum displays and promotes Caymanian artists and craftspeople, both established and grassroots. The gallery coordinates first-rate outreach programs for everyone from infants to inmates. It usually mounts six major exhibitions a year, including three large-scale retrospectives or thematic shows, and multimedia installations. Director Natalie Urquhart also brings in international shows that somehow relate to the island, often inviting local artists for stimulating dialogue. The gallery hosts public slide shows, a lunchtime lecture series in conjunction with current exhibits, Art Flix (video presentations on art history, introduced with a short lecture and followed by a discussion led by curators or artists), and a CineClub (movie night). The gallery has also developed an Artist Trail Map with the Department of Tourism and can facilitate studio tours. There's an excellent shop and an Art Café. ⊠ *Esterly Tibbetts Hwy. at Harquail Bypass, Seven Mile Beach* ☎ *345/945–8111* ⊕ *www. nationalgallery.org.ky* ⊠ *Free* ☉ *Closed Sun.*

CLOSE UP

Camana Bay

Dubbed a "new town" (in all senses of the term), ambitious in scope and philosophy, the mixed-use, master-planned Camana Bay stretches along 500 acres from Seven Mile Beach to the North Sound. It's a sustainable, traditional, and colorfully Caribbean—yet technologically cutting-edge—design, and ecologically sensitive to boot. Specifically designed by more than 100 consultants from several leading local and global firms as a gathering center to live, work, and play, Camana Bay has been carefully developed in three phases (the final phase is expected to be completed by 2019 and will include hotels and a marina, alongside residential and office development).

The four residential-office-retail courtyards feature unique color schemes unifying native flora with surrounding walls, walks, and mosaics. Streets were aligned to mitigate heat and to capture breezes. Plants were carefully chosen to attract birds and butterflies, and the development has green space galore, including artificial islands and harbors, as well as water features like canals and fountains.

The pedestrianized main street, called the Paseo, is lined with mostly high-end shops that are open late, restaurants, and entertainment (including a weekly farmers' market and a movie theater complex). The Paseo culminates in the Crescent, a waterfront plaza with restaurants, more gardens, interactive fountains, an esplanade, amphitheater, and public venues for fireworks to festivals. There are also jogging/biking trails, pocket parks, open spaces, and a beach. Residents and visitors are encouraged to park their cars and stroll (enhancing the green lifestyle) or just hang out.

WEST BAY

FAMILY **Cayman Turtle Centre.** Cayman's premier attraction has been transformed into a marine theme park with souvenir shops and restaurants. Still, the turtles remain a central attraction, and you can tour ponds in the original research–breeding facility with thousands in various stages of growth, some up to 600 pounds and more than 70 years old. Four areas—three aquatic and one dry—cover 23 acres; different-color bracelets determine access (the steep full-pass admission includes snorkeling gear and waterslides). The park helps promote conservation, encouraging interaction (a tidal pool houses invertebrates such as starfish and crabs) and observation. When turtles are picked up from the tanks, the little creatures flap their fins and splash the water. Animal

Program events include Keeper Talks, where you might feed birds or iguanas, and biologists' conservation programs. The freshwater **Breaker's Lagoon,** replete with cascades plunging over moss-carpeted rocks, evokes Cayman Brac. The saltwater **Boatswain's Lagoon,** replicating all the Cayman Islands and the Trench, teems with 14,000 denizens of the deep milling about a cannily designed synthetic reef. You can snorkel here (lessons and guided tours are available). Both lagoons have underwater 4-inch-thick acrylic panels that look directly into **Predator Reef,** home to six brown sharks, four nurse sharks, and other predatory fish such as tarpons, eels, and jacks, which can also be viewed from terra (or terror, as one guide jokes) firma. Look for feeding times. The free-flight **Aviary,** designed by consultants from Disney's Animal Kingdom, is a riot of color and noise with feathered friends representing the entire Caribbean basin; it doubles as a rehabilitation center for Cayman Wildlife and Rescue. A winding interpretive nature trail culminates in the **Blue Hole,** a collapsed cave once filled with water. Audio tours are available with different focuses, from butterflies to bush medicine. The last stop is the living museum, **Cayman Street,** with facades duplicating vernacular architecture. ⊠ *786 Northwest Point Rd., West Bay* ☎ *345/949–3894* ⊕ *www.turtle.ky* ⊠ *Comprehensive, $45; Turtle Farm only, $18.*

Hell. Quite literally the tourist trap from Hell, especially when overrun by cruise-ship passengers, this attraction does offer free admission, fun photo ops, and sublime surrealism. Its name refers to the quarter-acre of menacing shards of charred brimstone thrusting up like vengeful spirits (actually blackened and "sculpted" by acid-secreting algae and fungi over millennia). The eerie lunarscape is now cordoned off, but you can prove you had a helluva time by taking a photo from the observation deck. The attractions are the small post office and a gift shop where you can get cards and letters postmarked from Hell, not to mention wonderfully silly postcards titled "When Hell Freezes Over" (depicting bathing beauties on the beach), "The Devil Made Me Do It" bumper stickers, Scotch bonnet–based Hell sauce, and "The coolest shop in Hell" T-shirts. Ivan Farrington, the owner of the Devil's Hang-Out store, cavorts in a devil's costume (horn, cape, and tails), regaling you with demonically bad jokes. ⊠ *Hell Rd., West Bay* ☎ *345/949–3358* ⊠ *Free.*

EAST END AND NORTH SIDE

The Tourism Attraction Board and 14 leading eastern-district businesses (from Ocean Frontiers dive shop to Kaibo Beach Bar) and attractions developed the **"Discover the East" Adventure Card** to encourage visitors (and locals) to experience the beauty, culture, and heritage of Grand Cayman's eastern districts. The $20 card provides free admission to the Queen Elizabeth II Botanic Park and to Pedro St. James (normally CI$10 each), as well as gifts and discounts throughout Bodden Town, Cayman Kai, North Side, and the East End, from free desserts with dinner to $20 off diving.

FAMILY **Blowholes.** When the easterly trade winds blow hard, crashing waves force water into caverns and send impressive geysers shooting up as much as 20 feet through the ironshore. The blowholes were partially filled during Hurricane Ivan in 2004, so the water must be rough to recapture their former elemental drama. ✉ *Frank Sound Rd., roughly 10 miles (16 km) east of Bodden Town, near East End.*

Bodden Town. In the island's original south-shore capital you can find an old cemetery on the shore side of the road. Graves with A-frame structures are said to contain the remains of pirates. There are also the ruins of a fort and a wall erected by slaves in the 19th century. The National Trust runs tours of the restored 1840s Mission House.

Cayman Islands Brewery. In this brewery occupying the former Stingray facility, tour guides explain the iconic imagery of bottle and label as well as the nearly three-week brewing process: 7 days' fermentation, 10 days' lagering (storage), and 1 day in the bottling tank. The brewery's ecofriendly features are also championed: local farmers receive the spent grains to feed their cattle at no charge, while waste liquid is channeled into one of the Caribbean's most advanced water-treatment systems. Then, enjoy your complimentary tasting knowing that you're helping the local environment and economy. The little shop also offers cute merchandise and a happening happy hour that lures locals for liming (as a sign prominently chides: "No working during drinking hours"). ✉ *366 Shamrock Rd., Prospect* ☎ *345/947–6699* ⊕ *cib.ky* ✉ *$6.*

★ Fodor'sChoice **Crystal Caves.** At the end of a seemingly end-
FAMILY less, bumpy road, your guide takes you on a short hike to the "treehouse" refreshment-souvenir stand of this Grand

DID YOU KNOW?

The blowholes on Grand Cayman's south shore were formed when waves pushed seawater through the ceilings of caves under the ironshore, sending the spray up into the air.

Cayman House and Garden

The few original Caymanian cottages that exist represent a unique architectural vernacular cannily adapted to the climate and available resources. Foundation posts and floors were constructed from durable, termite-resistant ironwood. Wattle-and-daub walls were fashioned from basket-woven sticks plastered on both sides with lime daub (extracted coral burned with various woods). The earliest roofs were thatched with woven palm fronds (later shingled or topped with corrugated zinc); their peaks helped cool houses, as hot air rises. The kitchen was separate, usually just a "caboose" stove for cooking.

The other unusual custom, "backing sand," originated as a Christmas tradition, then became a year-round decorative statement. Women and children would tote woven-thatch baskets by moonlight to the beach, bringing "back" glittering white sand to cover their front yards. They'd rake intricate patterns and adorn the sand with sinuous conch-shell paths. The yard was also swept Saturday so it would look well tended after Sunday services. A side benefit was that it helped reduce insect infestation.

Cayman locale. A viewing platform provides breathtaking vistas of a ginormous banyan tree framing the first cave entrance. Currently, three large caverns in the extensive network have been opened and outfitted with wood pathways and strategic lighting. Millions of years ago, the network was submerged underwater (a subterranean lake serves as a hauntingly lovely reminder); the land gradually rose over millennia. Nature has fashioned extraordinary crystal gardens and "fish-scale" columns from delicate, fragile flowstone; part of the fun is identifying the fanciful shapes whimsically carved by the stalactites and stalagmites. The 90-minute tours are offered on the hour from 9 am through 4 pm. Ambitious plans include adding ziplines and 4WD trails. If you're going on to tour the East End, look for the fascinating little Davidoff's sculpture garden (depicting local critters) along the coastal highway just outside the caves. ⊠ *69 Northside Rd., Old Man Bay* ☎ *345/949–2283, 345/925–3001* ⊕ *www.caymancrystalcaves.com* ⊠ *$40.*

★ **Fodor's**Choice **Pedro St. James Castle.** Built in 1780, the great house is Cayman's oldest stone structure and the island's only remaining late-18th-century residence. In its capacity as courthouse and jail, it was the birthplace of Caymanian

Pedro St. James Castle

democracy, where in December 1831 the first elected parliament was organized and in 1835 the Slavery Abolition Act signed. The structure still has original or historically accurate replicas of sweeping verandahs, mahogany floors, rough-hewn wide-beam ceilings, outside louvers, stone and oxblood- or mustard-color lime-wash-painted walls, brass fixtures, and Georgian furnishings (from tea caddies to canopy beds to commodes). Paying obsessive attention to detail, the curators even fill glasses with faux wine. The minimuseum also includes a hodgepodge of displays from slave emancipation to old stamps. The buildings are surrounded by 8 acres of natural parks and woodlands. You can stroll through landscaping of native Caymanian flora and experience one of the most spectacular views on the island from atop the dramatic Great Pedro Bluff. First watch the impressive multimedia show, on the hour, complete with smoking pots, misting rains, and two screens. The poignant Hurricane Ivan Memorial outside uses text, images, and symbols to represent important aspects of the 2004 disaster. A branch of Cayman Spirits brings history further to life with rum tastings. ⊠ *305 Pedro Castle Rd., Savannah* ☎ *345/947–3329* ⊕ *www.pedrostjames.ky* ⊠ *CI$10.*

★ Fodor's Choice **Queen Elizabeth II Botanic Park.** This 65-acre wilderness preserve showcases a wide range of indigenous and nonindigenous tropical vegetation, approximately 2,000 species in total. Splendid sections include numerous water

FAMILY

features from limpid lily ponds to cascades; a Heritage Garden with a traditional cottage and "caboose" (outside kitchen) that includes crops that might have been planted on Cayman a century ago; and a Floral Colour Garden arranged by color, the walkway wandering through sections of pink, red, orange, yellow, white, blue, mauve, lavender, and purple. A 2-acre lake and adjacent wetlands include three islets that provide a habitat and breeding ground for native birds just as showy as the floral displays: green herons, black-necked stilts, American coots, blue-winged teal, cattle egrets, and rare West Indian whistling ducks. The nearly mile-long Woodland Trail encompasses every Cayman ecosystem from wetland to cactus thicket, button-wood swamp to lofty woodland with imposing mahogany trees. You'll encounter birds, lizards, turtles, and agoutis, but the park's star residents are the protected endemic blue iguanas, found only in Grand Cayman. The world's most endangered iguana, they're the focus of the National Trust's Blue Iguana Recovery Program, a captive breeding and reintroduction facility. This section of the park is usually closed to the public, though released "blue dragons" hang out in the vicinity. The Trust conducts 90-minute behind-the-scenes safaris Monday–Saturday at 11 am for $30. ✉ *367 Botanic Rd., North Side* ☎ *345/947–9462* ⊕ *www. botanic-park.ky* ▣ *CI$10.*

Wreck of the Ten Sails Park. This lonely, lovely park on Grand Cayman's windswept eastern tip commemorates the island's most (in)famous shipwreck. On February 8, 1794, the *Cordelia,* heading a convoy of 58 square-rigged merchant vessels en route from Jamaica to England, foundered on one of the treacherous East End reefs. Its warning cannon fire was tragically misconstrued as a call to band more closely together due to imminent pirate attack, and nine more ships ran aground. Local sailors, who knew the rough seas, demonstrated great bravery in rescuing all 400-odd seamen. Popular legend claims (romantically but inaccurately) that King George III granted the islands·an eternal tax exemption. Queen Elizabeth II dedicated the park's plaque in 1994. Interpretive signs document the historic details. The ironically peaceful headland provides magnificent views of the reef (including more recent shipwrecks); bird-watching is superb from here half a mile south along the coast to the Lighthouse Park, perched on a craggy bluff. ✉ *Gun Bay, East End* ☎ *345/949–0121 National Trust* ▣ *Free.*

Queen Elizabeth II Botanic Park

SHOPPING

There's no sales tax, and there is plenty of duty-free merchandise on Grand Cayman, including jewelry, china, crystal, perfumes, and cameras. Savings on luxury goods range between 10% and 25%. Notable exceptions are liquor, which is available minus that tariff only at specially designated shops, and haute couture (though the ritzier resort shops stock some designer labels). "Brand Cayman" is the local nickname for the glamorous shops along Cardinal Avenue, the local answer to New York's Madison Avenue and Beverly Hills's Rodeo Drive. Esteemed names include Cartier, Waterford, and Wedgwood.

Worthy local items include woven thatch mats and baskets, coconut soap, hardwood carvings, jewelry made from a marblelike stone called Caymanite (from Cayman Brac's cliffs, a striated amalgam of several metals), and authentic sunken treasure often fashioned into jewelry, though the last is never cheap (request a certificate of authenticity if one isn't offered). You'll also find individual artists' ateliers and small, colorful craft shops whose owners often love discussing the old days and traditions. Bear in mind that most major attractions feature extensive and/or intriguing gift shops, whether at the Turtle Centre, National Trust, or the National Gallery.

Blue Dragons

CLOSE UP

Cosponsored by the Botanic Park and the National Trust, the **Blue Iguana Recovery Program** (⊕ www.blueiguana.ky) is a model captive breeding plan for the remarkable reptiles that only two decades ago faced total extinction. The Grand Cayman blue iguana lived on the island for millennia until man arrived, its only natural predator the racer snake. Until recently they were the world's most critically endangered species, functionally extinct with only 25 remaining in the wild. BIRP has released more than 300 into the Salina Reserve, with an ultimate repopulation goal of 1,000 if they can breed successfully in the wild.

The National Trust conducts safaris six mornings a week, giving you a chance to see hatchlings in the cages, camouflaged toddlers, and breeding-age adults like Mad Max and Blue Blue. Most of the iguanas raised here are released at two years by the Wildlife Conservation Society with a microchip implant tag for radio tracking and color-coded beading for unique identification. Tones fluctuate according to lighting and season, brightening to azure during the April–May breeding period. Guides explain the gestation and incubation periods and the pairing of potential mates. Sadly, you'll also learn why the breeding program is on temporary hiatus: a mysterious bacterium affecting the blues.

If you can't make it to the park, look for the 15 larger-than-life, one-of-a-kind outdoor sculptures commissioned from local artists scattered around the island. You can download maps of the Blue Dragon Trail from the BIRP, National Trust, and Botanic Park sites. Many hotels also stock leaflets with maps and fun facts (the iguanas live up to 70 years, grow to 6 feet in length, and weigh 25 pounds). You can even purchase custom blue iguana products (helping fund research), such as Joel Friesch's limited-edition hand-painted bobbleheads (blues bob their heads rapidly as a territorial warning) packaged in a bright-yellow, hard cardboard box. You can also volunteer for a working vacation (or longer fieldwork study stint) online.

Local palate pleasers include treats made by the Tortuga Rum Company (both the famed cakes and the actual distilled spirit, including a sublime 12-year-old rum), Cayman Honey, Cayman Taffy, and Cayman Sea Salt (from the ecofriendly "farm" of the same name). Seven Fathoms is the first working distillery actually in Cayman itself, its award-winning rums aged underwater (hence the name). Also seek out such gastronomic goodies as jams, sauces, and vinegars from Hawley Haven and Whistling Duck Farms on the eastern half of the island. Cigar lovers, take note: Some shops carry famed Cuban brands, but you must enjoy them on the island; bringing them back to the United States is illegal.

An almost unbroken line of strip malls runs from George Town through Seven Mile Beach, most of them presenting shopping and dining options galore. The ongoing Camana Bay mega-development already glitters with glam shops, including Island Companies' largest and grandest store offering the hautest name-brand jewelry, watches, and duty-free goods.

GEORGE TOWN

SHOPPING CENTERS

Bayshore Mall. Optimally located downtown and one of the leading shopaholics' targets (you can't miss the cotton-candy colors), this mall contains a Kirk Freeport department-store branch (Tag Heuer to Herend porcelain, Mikimoto to Mont Blanc), swank Lalique and Lladró boutiques, La Parfumerie (which often offers makeovers and carries 450 beauty brands), and other usual luxury culprits. ⊠ *S. Church St., George Town.*

Cayside Courtyard. This small courtyard shopping center is noted for its specialty jewelers and antiques dealers. ⊠ *Harbour Dr., George Town.*

Duty Free Plaza. This mall caters to more casual shoppers with the T-shirt Factory, Island Treasures, Havana Cigars, Blackbeard's Rumcake Bakery, and the Surf Shop. It also contains a kid-pleasing 12,000-gallon saltwater aquarium with sharks, eels, and stingrays. ⊠ *S. Church St., George Town.*

Island Plaza. Here you'll find 15 duty- and tax-free stores, including Swarovski Boutique, Island Jewellers, and Churchill's Cigars (with bars like Margaritaville to de-stress in after binge shopping). ⊠ *Harbour Dr., George Town.*

Kirk Freeport Plaza. This downtown shopping center, home to the Kirk Freeport flagship department store, is ground zero for couture; it's also known for its boutiques selling fine watches and jewelry, china, crystal, leather, perfumes, and cosmetics, from Baccarat to Bulgari, Raymond Weil

Words and Music

Local books and CDs make wonderful gifts and souvenirs. Recapture the flavor of your stay with *Miss Cleo's Cayman Kitchen*—subtitled "Treasured Recipes from the East End"—by Cleopatra Conolly, or *Cook' in Little Cayman,* by irrepressible Gladys Howard, a longtime resort owner who studied under James Beard and Julia Child. Plunge into *Diary of a Dirtbag Divemaster* by Little Cayman's Terry Thompson; it's a fact-inspired fiction recounting the escapades of six dive instructors working on a small Caribbean island. Another Little Cayman expat, Gay Morse, relates her own amusing behind-the-scenes anecdotes about teaching scuba and helping operate a small resort, *So You Want to Live on an Island?* H. George "Barefoot Man" Nowak's *Which Way to the Islands?* is another hilarious collection of only-in-the-Caribbean stories. Noted artist Nasaria Suck-

oo-Chollette pens poems and short stories based on local culture and folklore, including *Story Telling Rundown.* On a more serious note, celebrated photographer Courtney Platt documented the devastation wrought by Hurricane Ivan in the 330 striking images composing *Paradise Interrupted.*

Sway back home to soca, reggae, calypso, and Carib-country beats. Grand Cayman has several recording studios, including the state-of-the-art Hopscotch, whose Platinum label records both Lammie and MOJ. Garden Studios is owned by popular group Hi Tide. C and B Studio records exclusively for Sea and B—Earl la Pierre and Barefoot Man (the latter alone has 28 CDs and counting). Other worthwhile local recording artists include jazz masters Gary Ebanks and Intransit, hard rockers Ratskyn and Cloudburst, and sultry soulster Karen Edie.

---

to Waterford and Wedgwood (the last two share their own autonomous boutique). Just keep walking—there's plenty of eye-catching, mind-boggling consumerism in all directions: Boucheron, Cartier (with its own mini-boutique), Chanel, Clinique, Christian Dior, Clarins, Estée Lauder, Fendi, Guerlain, Lancôme, Yves Saint Laurent, Issey Miyake, Jean Paul Gaultier, Nina Ricci, Rolex, Roberto Coin, Rosenthal and Royal Doulton china, and more. ⊠ *Cardinal Ave., George Town.*

Landmark. Stores in the Landmark sell perfumes, treasure coins, and upscale beachwear; Breezes Bistro restaurant is upstairs. ⊠ *Harbour Dr., George Town.*

ART GALLERIES

The art scene has exploded in the past decade, moving away from typical Caribbean motifs and "primitive" styles. Cayman's most famous artist had been the late Gladwyn Bush, fondly known as Miss Lassie, who died in 2003. She began painting her intuitive religious subjects after a vision she had when she was 62. She also decorated the facade, interior walls, furnishings, even appliances of her home, which was converted into a museum and workshop space, The Mind's Eye, at the junction of South Shore Road and Walkers Road. Bush was awarded the MBE (Most Excellent Order of the British Empire) in 1997, and her work is found in collections from Paris to Baltimore, the latter of whose American Visionary Art Museum owns several canvases. Bendel Hydes is another widely respected local, who moved to SoHo more than two decades ago yet still paints Caymanian-inspired works that capture the islands' elemental colors and dynamic movement. Leading expat artists include Joanne Sibley and Charles Long, both of whom create more figurative Cayman-focused art, from luminous landscapes and shining portraits to pyrotechnically hued flora. Several artists' home-studios double as galleries, including the internationally known Al Ebanks, the controversial Luelan Bodden, and fanciful sculptor Horacio Esteban; the National Gallery has a full list.

Al Ebanks Studio Gallery. This gallery shows the eponymous artist's versatile, always provocative work in various media. Because you're walking into his home as well as atelier, everything is on display. Clever movable panels maximize space "like art Murphy beds." His work, while inspired by his home, could never be labeled traditional Caribbean art, exhibiting vigorous movement through abstract swirls of color and textural contrasts. Though nonrepresentational (save for his equally intriguing sculpture and ceramics), the focal subject from carnivals to iguanas is always subtly apparent. Ask him about the Native Sons art movement he cofounded. ⊠ *186B Shedden Rd., George Town* ☏ *345/927–5365, 345/949–0693.*

Artifacts. On the George Town waterfront, Artifacts sells Spanish pieces of eight, doubloons, and Halcyon Days enamels (hand-painted collectible pillboxes made in England), as well as antique maps and other collectibles. ⊠ *Cayside Courtyard, Harbour Dr., George Town* ☏ *345/949–2442* ⊕ *www.artifacts.com.ky.*

Native Sons: Caymanian Artists

In 1995 three artists founded a collaborative called Native Sons, adding a fourth in 1996, and currently featuring 10 members. Their primary goal is to develop and promote Caymanian artists. Though they work in different mediums and styles, the group resists facile characterization and challenges conventions as to what characterizes "Caribbean" art. One of the core members, Al Ebanks, has achieved major international success, but he admits that the islands can be provincial: "Cayman doesn't always recognize talent unless you're signed to a gallery overseas."

Though the National Gallery and the Cayman National Cultural Foundation both vigorously support the movement and are committed to sponsoring local artists, some Native Sons members feel their agendas can be too safe, ironically exemplifying the bureaucratic, corporate mentality they admit is often necessary to raise funds for nonprofit institutions. They have also felt subtle pressure to conform commercially and an inherent bias toward expat artists, whose work often depicts the literally sunnier side of Caymanian life, and resent what they perceived to be censorship of rawer, edgier works, including depictions of nudity in archconservative Cayman. They have sought to push the boundaries for both institutions and private galleries. "Yes, art is art and shouldn't be grounded in national stereotypes, though my country inspires my work. ... We just want balance," Ebanks says. "People look at more challenging work and ask 'Where are the boats?' We live that scene!"

Obviously this is a hot-button topic on a tiny island. Chris Christian, who originally achieved success through representational beach scenes but wanted to expand and experiment, uses the Cayman term "crabs in a bucket," describing how "artists in a small pool scratch and scramble over each other, succeeding by badmouthing others." Which is why the support structure and philosophy of Native Sons is so vital: They help each other negotiate "that constant balance between commercial success and artistic integrity."

Other members include cofounder Wray Banker, Randy Chollette, Nasaria Suckoo-Chollette, Gordon Solomon, Horacio Esteban, and Nickola McCoy. These native sons and daughters all passionately believe art isn't merely about pretty pictures, and uncompromisingly believe in preserving Caymanian culture and freedom of expression.

Cathy Church's Underwater Photo Centre and Gallery. The store has a collection of the acclaimed underwater shutterbug's spectacular color and limited-edition black-and-white underwater photos as well as the latest marine camera equipment. Cathy will autograph her latest coffee-table book, talk about her globe-trotting adventures, and schedule private underwater photography instruction on her dive boat, with graphics-oriented computers to critique your work. She also does wedding photography, above and underwater. If you can't stop in, check out the world's largest underwater photo installation (9 by 145 feet) at the Owen Roberts Airport baggage claim, curated by Cathy and her team. ⊠ *390 S. Church St., George Town* ☎ *345/949–7415* ⊕ *www.cathychurch.com.*

Cayman Spirits/Seven Fathoms Rum. Surprisingly, this growing company, established in 2008, is Cayman's first distillery. It's already garnered medals in prestigious international competitions for its artisanal small-batch rums (and is now making a splash for its smooth Gun Bay vodka as well). You can stop by for a tasting and self-guided tour (a more intensive, extensive guided tour costs $15) to learn how the rum is aged at 7 fathoms (42 feet) deep; supposedly the natural motion of the currents maximizes the rum's contact with the oak, extracting its rich flavors and enhancing complexity. ⊠ *65 Bronze Rd., George Town* ☎ *345/925–5379, 345/926–8186* ⊕ *www.caymanspirits. com, www.sevenfathomsrum.com.*

Guy Harvey's Gallery and Shoppe. World-renowned marine biologist, conservationist, and artist Guy Harvey showcases his aquatic-inspired, action-packed art in every conceivable medium, from tableware to sportswear (even logo soccer balls and Zippos). The soaring, two-story 4,000-square-foot space is almost more theme park than store, with monitors playing sport-fishing videos, wood floors inlaid with tile duplicating rippling water, dangling catboats "attacked" by shark models, and life-size murals honoring such classics as Hemingway's *Old Man and the Sea.* Original paintings, sculpture, and drawings are expensive, but there's something (tile art, prints, lithographs, and photos) in most price ranges. ⊠ *49 S. Church St., George Town* ☎ *345/943–4891* ⊕ *www.guyharvey.com.*

Pure Art. About 1½ miles (2½ km) south of George Town, Pure Art purveys wit, warmth, and whimsy from the wildly colored front steps. Its warren of rooms resembles a garage sale run amok or a quirky grandmother's attic spilling over with unexpected finds, from foodstuffs to functional and wearable art. ⊠ *S. Church St. and Denham-Thompson Way, George Town* ☎ *345/949–9133* ⊕ *www.pureart.ky.*

CAMERAS

Camera Store. This store has friendly and knowledgeable service, lots of duty-free digital cameras, accessories, and fast photo printing from self-service kiosks. ⊠ *32 Goring Ave., George Town* ☎ *345/949–8359.*

CIGARS

Given Cayman's proximity to Cuba, the banned but tempting panatelas and robustos are readily available at reasonable prices. They are still considered contraband in the United States until the embargo is lifted.

Churchill's Cigars. A cigar-store Indian points the way into this tobacco emporium, which sells the island's largest selection of authentic Cubanos (and other imports), including such names as Upmann, Romeo y Julieta, and Cohiba, displayed in the dark, clubby surroundings. The enthusiastic staff will advise on drink pairings (bold older rum for a Montecristo No. 2, cognac for smaller Partagas Shorts, a single-malt scotch such as Glenmorangie for the Bolivar Belicoso Fino). There's a small airport branch as well. ⊠ *Island Plaza, Harbour Dr., George Town* ☎ *345/945–6141* ⊕ *www.islandcompaniesltd.com/stores/churchills-cigars.*

CLOTHING

Arabus. The store carries casual and classy pieces by everyone from Karan to Kors. ⊠ *42 Edward St., George Town* ☎ *345/949–4620* ⊕ *www.arabus.org.*

Blue Wave. At this surf and clothing shop you'll find brands like Billabong, Quicksilver, and Olukai, plus essentials like sandals, sunglasses, and surfboards. ⊠ *10 Shedden Rd., George Town* ☎ *345/949–8166.*

FOODSTUFFS

There are seven modern, U.S.-style supermarkets (three of them have full-service pharmacies) on Grand Cayman. Ask for the one nearest you. Together, they will spoil you for choices of fresh fruit and vegetables, a wide selection of groceries, and a good selection of meats, poultry, and fish. All have deli counters serving hot meals, salads, sandwiches, cold cuts, and cheeses. Kirk Supermarket carries a wide range of international foods from the Caribbean, Europe, and Asia. The biggest difference you'll find between these

and supermarkets on the mainland is the prices, which are about 25%–30% more than at home.

Foster's Food Fair-IGA. The island's biggest chain has five supermarkets. The Airport Centre and Strand stores, with full-service pharmacies, are open Monday–Saturday 7 am–11 pm. ⊠ *Airport Centre, 63 Dorcy Dr., George Town* ☎ *345/949–5155, 345/945–3663* ⊕ *www.fosters-iga.com.*

Kirk Supermarket and Pharmacy. This store is open Monday–Thursday 7 am–10 pm (11 pm Friday and Saturday) and is a particularly good source for traditional Caymanian fast food (oxtail, curried goat) and beverages at the juice bar. It also carries the largest selection of organic and special dietary products; the pharmacy (Monday–Saturday 8 am–9 pm) stocks homeopathic and herbal remedies. ⊠ *413 Eastern Ave., near intersection with West Bay Rd., George Town* ☎ *345/949–7022* ⊕ *www.kirkmarket.ky.*

Tortuga Rum Company. This company bakes, then vacuum-seals more than 10,000 of its world-famous rum cakes daily, adhering to the original, "secret" century-old recipe. There are eight flavors, from banana to Blue Mountain coffee; the new taffy also comes in eight varieties. The 12-year-old rum, blended from private stock though actually distilled in Guyana, is a connoisseur's delight for after-dinner sipping. You can buy a fresh rum cake at the airport on the way home at the same prices as at the factory store. ⊠ *Industrial Park, N. Sound Rd., George Town* ☎ *345/943–7663* ⊕ *www.tortugarumcakes.com.*

HANDICRAFTS AND SOUVENIRS

Pirate's Grotto. This small store offers duty-free liquor and cigars (including Cubans) as well as Cayman Islands souvenirs. ⊠ *Harbour Dr., basement level, below Landmark Shopping Center, George Town* ☎ *345/945–0244.*

JEWELRY

Although you can find black-coral products in Grand Cayman, they're controversial. Most of the coral sold here comes from Belize and Honduras; Cayman Islands marine law prohibits the removal of live coral from its own sea. Black coral grows at a glacial rate (3 inches per decade) and is an endangered species. Cayman, however, is famed for artisans working with the material; shops are recommended, but let your conscience dictate your purchases.

Balaclava Jewellers. This shop is the domain of Martina and Philip Cadien, who studied at Germany's prestigious

CLOSE UP

Guy Harvey

Guy Harvey is a man of many hats. He has a PhD in marine biology and is also a world-class angler, author, renowned aquatic wildlife artist, cinematographer, TV producer, presenter of a former weekly TV program titled *Portraits from the Deep,* clothing designer, and dedicated environmentalist.

Anyone passing through the Fort Lauderdale airport has seen his dramatic three-story mural (a smaller mural may once again adorn Grand Cayman's Owen Roberts Airport). His art features meticulous composition and vibrant color, capturing the adrenaline-pumping action. "I try to humanize them, give them character in my paintings," Harvey says, though hardly in dewy, Disney-esque fashion.

Growing up a 10th-generation Jamaican, he loved fishing and diving with his father from an early age. Obsessed by all things aquatic, Harvey first gained notice in art circles with a 1985 Kingston exhibit of pen-and-ink drawings based on Hemingway's *Old Man and the Sea,* a recurring theme: man and animal bonding and exhibiting grace under pressure in their struggle for survival.

He moved to Cayman during Jamaica's political upheaval in the late 1970s. He liked Cayman's similar culture and cuisine, British heritage, and proximity to both Jamaica and Florida. Harvey has used his high profile together with his skills as an artist, angler, author, and documentarian to strike merchandising deals, creating apparel, a line of housewares, and restaurants, and pouring many of the profits back into research. He still travels the world on interactive marine programs.

Harvey has consistently supported "catch and release" ethics for game fish around the world. He works closely with many conservation organizations to help protect global fishery resources and was appointed a trustee of the International Game Fish Association in 1992; six years later he was voted the IGFA's first-ever Lifetime Achievement Award from the World Fishing Awards Committee. The nonprofit Guy Harvey Research Institute was established with the Oceanographic Center of Nova Southeastern University in 1999 to support effective conservation and restoration of fish resources and biodiversity. His views can be controversial. Commenting on dolphin swim programs, he has said: "Dolphin safety is one of the biggest lies foisted on the public."

Pforzheim Goldsmithing School. The showroom sparkles appropriately, with breathtaking handcrafted pieces—usually naturally colored diamonds set in platinum or 18K white, yellow, and rose gold—framed and lovingly, almost sensuously lit. Although there are simpler strands, this is a place where flash holds sway; the prices take your breath away, but the gaudy gems are flawless. ⊠ *Governors Square, 23 Lime Tree Bay Ave., Seven Mile Beach* ☎ *345/945–5788* ⊕ *www.balaclava-jewellers.com.*

Island Time. Locals appreciate Island Time for its affordable line of watches, especially top-notch Swiss brands, from Movado to Marvin to Maurice Lacroix. There's another branch with similar inventory in the Flagship Building. ⊠ *Island Plaza, Cardinal Ave., George Town* ☎ *345/946–2333* ⊕ *www.islandcompaniesltd.com/stores/island-time.*

Magnum Jewelers. Befitting its name, Magnum Jewelers traffics in high-caliber pieces by the elite likes of Girard-Perregeaux and Harry Winston for a high-powered clientele. President Harry Chandi travels the world, his keen eye sourcing distinctive contemporary watches and bijoux (especially increasingly rare colored diamonds) for his equally glittery celebrity clientele, who appreciate a bargain like the rest of us. Smaller spenders might appreciate whimsical items such as pendants with hand-painted enamel sandals or crystal-encrusted purses. ⊠ *Cardinal Plaza, Cardinal Ave., George Town* ☎ *345/946–9199* ⊕ *www.magnumjewelers.com.*

SEVEN MILE BEACH

SHOPPING CENTERS

Galleria Plaza. Nicknamed Blue Plaza for its azure hue, Galleria Plaza features several galleries and exotic home-accessories stores dealing in Oriental rugs or Indonesian furnishings, as well as more moderate souvenir shops hawking T-shirts and swimwear. ⊠ *West Bay Rd., Seven Mile Beach.*

The Strand Shopping Centre. This mall has branches of Tortuga Rum and Blackbeard's Liquor, Polo Ralph Lauren and another Kirk Freeport (this location is particularly noteworthy for china and crystal, from Kosta Boda to Baccarat, as well as a second La Parfumerie). You'll also find banks galore so you can withdraw cash. ⊠ *West Bay Rd., Seven Mile Beach.*

Cayman Craft Market

This open-air marketplace run by the Tourism Attraction Board at Hog Sty Bay, smack in the middle of George Town, is artist central, helping maintain old-time Caymanian skills. The vendors offer locally made leather, thatch, wood, and shell items. You'll also find dolls, hats, carved parrots, bead and seed jewelry, hand-painted thatch bags and bonnets, and hand-carved waurie (also spelled warri) boards—an ancient African game using seeds or (more modernly) marbles.

Also available here are Sea Salt (and their luxury bath product);

Hawley Haven Farm products (Mrs. Laurie Hawley's delectable papaya, tamarind, and guava jams; spicy mango chutney; thyme vinegar; Cayman honey; and jerk sauce; as well as her painted folkloric characters on handmade sundried paper made with native flowers, leaves, and herbs); the Cayman Tropicals line of fragrant fruit-based hair and skin-care products; and North Side's Whistling Duck Farm specialties, from soursop to sea grape jams and jellies. Every month highlights a different area of the Cayman Islands, from Cayman Brac to Bodden Town.

West Shore Shopping Centre. Dubbed Pink Plaza for reasons that become obvious upon approach, West Shore offers upscale boutiques and galleries (tenants range from Sotheby's International Realty to the Body Shop). ⊠ *West Bay Rd., Seven Mile Beach.*

ART GALLERIES

Ritz-Carlton Gallery. This gallery more than fulfilled one of the resort's conditions upon securing rights to build, which was to commission local arts and artisans to help decorate the public spaces. The corridor-cum-bridge spanning West Bay Road became a gallery where Chris Christian of Cayman Traditional Arts curates quarterly exhibitions of Cayman's finest (there are also themed shows devoted to photography and local kids' art). Each piece is for sale; CTA or the hotel will mediate in the negotiations between artist and buyer at a favorable commission. ⊠ *Ritz-Carlton Grand Cayman, West Bay Rd., Seven Mile Beach* ☎ *345/943–9000, 345/926–0119.*

BOOKS

Books & Books. The Miami independent bookseller operates this outlet in Grand Cayman. Regular events include
author readings and "Floetry," when poets and performers
express themselves at the open mike. An entire room is
devoted to kids with toys, educational games, and books
from toddler to YA; twice-weekly story and craft time
keep them occupied while parents browse. ⊠ *45 Market
St., Camana Bay* ☎*345/640–2665* ⊕*www.booksandbooks.
com/grandcayman.*

CIGARS

Havana Club Cigars. This store is the brainchild of Raglan
Roper, who sailed from Florida to Cayman, stopping in
Cuba en route. Immediately hooked on the cigars, cuisine,
and culture, he eventually opened a Cayman shop, then
expanded (he also owns a Cuban restaurant). In addition to the famed brands, the attraction is the irresistible
in-house *torcedor* (cigar roller), Jesus Lara Perez, who
rotates demonstrations between the stores. Jesus started
working at 14 in the Cuban cigar factory La Isolina in
Santa Clara, eventually becoming chief cigar roller for
other leading brands. ⊠ *West Shore Center, 508 West Bay
Rd., Seven Mile Beach* ☎*345/946–0523, 345/946–5396*
⊕*www.clubhavanacayman.com.*

JEWELRY

Mitzi's Fine Jewelry. Mitzi's is a treasure trove of salvaged
18th-century coins, silver, Caymanite pieces, and black
coral; the store also carries Italian porcelain and the Carrera
y Carrera line of jewelry and sculptures. Self-taught, viva-
cious proprietor Mitzi Callan, who specializes in handmade
pieces, is usually on hand to help. She also heads the Starvin'
Artists co-op and opened an intriguing local organic cos-
metics/toiletries store next door. ⊠ *5 Bay Harbour Centre,
West Bay Rd., Seven Mile Beach* ☎*345/945–5014.*

WHERE TO EAT IN GRAND CAYMAN

Updated
by Jordan
Simon

NO INDIGENOUS PEOPLES OR GAGGLE of contentious colonial powers left much of an imprint on Grand Cayman cuisine, as was the case on many other islands. Until recently, the strongest culinary contributions to Cayman cuisine came from nearby Jamaica and, to a lesser extent, Cuba, though the worst of the British pub tradition lingered in pasties and heavy puddings. Fortunately, since the boom of the late 1970s, chefs from around the world (and the influx of expats from as far afield as Beijing and Berlin) have seasoned a once-bland dining scene.

Today, despite its small size, comparative isolation, and British colonial trappings, Grand Cayman offers a smorgasbord of gastronomic goodies. With more than 100 eateries, something should suit and sate every palate and pocketbook (especially once you factor in fast-food franchises sweeping the islandscape like tumbleweed and stalls dispensing local specialties).

The term *melting pot* describes both the majority of menus and the multicultural population. It's not uncommon to find "American" dishes at an otherwise Caribbean restaurant, Indian fare at an Italian eatery (and vice versa). The sheer range of dining options from Middle Eastern to Mexican reflects the island's cosmopolitan, discriminating clientele. Imported ingredients reflect the United Nations, with chefs sourcing salmon from Norway, foie gras from Périgord, and lamb from New Zealand. Wine lists can be equally global in scope (often receiving awards from such oeno-bibles as *Wine Spectator*). Don't be surprised to find both Czech and Chilean staffers at a remote East End restaurant.

WHERE TO EAT

Grand Cayman dining is casual (even shorts are okay, at least for lunch, but *not* beachwear and tank tops). More upscale restaurants usually require slacks for dinner. Mosquitoes can be pesky when you dine outdoors, especially at sunset, so plan ahead or ask for repellent. Winter can be chilly enough to warrant a light sweater. You should make reservations at all but the most casual places, particularly during the high season.

Since nearly everything must be imported, prices average about 25% higher than those in a major U.S. city. Many restaurants add a 10%–15% service charge to the bill; be sure to check before leaving a tip (waiters usually receive

Eat Like a Local

CLOSE UP

Caymanian cuisine evolved from whatever could be coaxed from the sea and eked out from the poor, porous soil. Farmers cultivated carb-rich crops that could remain fresh without refrigeration and furnish energy for the heavy labor typical of the islanders' hardscrabble existence. Hence pumpkins, coconuts, plantains, breadfruit, sweet potatoes, yams, and other "provisions" (root vegetables) became staple ingredients. Turtle (now farm-raised), the traditional specialty, can be served in soup or stew and as a steak. Conch, the meat of a large pink mollusk, is prepared in stews, chowders, and fritters, and panfried (cracked). Fish—including snapper, tuna, wahoo, grouper, and marlin—is served baked, broiled, steamed, or "Cayman style" (as an *escovitch* with peppers, onions, and tomatoes).

"Rundown" is another classic: Fish (marinated with fresh lime juice, scallions, and fiery Scotch bonnet peppers) is steamed in coconut milk with breadfruit, pumpkin dumplings, and/ or cassava. Fish tea boils and bubbles similar ingredients for hours—even days—until it thickens into gravy. The traditional dessert, heavy cake, earned its name because excluding scarce flour and eggs made it incredibly dense: Coconut, sugar, spices, and butter are boiled, mixed with seasonal binders (cassava, yam, pumpkin), and baked.

Jamaican influence is seen in oxtail, goat stew, jerk chicken and pork, salt cod, and ackee (a red tree fruit resembling scrambled eggs in flavor and texture when cooked), and manish water (a lusty goat-head stew with garlic, thyme, scallion, green banana [i.e., plantain], yam, potato, and other tubers).

only a small portion of any included gratuities, so leave something extra at your discretion for good service). Alcohol can send your meal tab skyrocketing. Buy liquor duty-free, either at the airport before your flight to the Cayman Islands or in one of the duty-free liquor stores that can be found in almost every strip mall on Grand Cayman, and enjoy a cocktail or nightcap from the comfort of your room or balcony. Cayman customs limits you to two bottles per person. Lunch often offers the same or similar dishes at a considerable discount. Finally, when you are figuring your dining budget, remember that the Cayman dollar is worth 25% more than the U.S. dollar, and virtually all menus are priced in Cayman dollars.

Restaruant reviews have been shortened. For full information, visit Fodors.com

WHAT IT COSTS IN U.S. DOLLARS			
$	$$	$$$	$$$$
Restaurants under $12	$12–$20	$21–$30	over $30

Prices in the restaurant reviews are the average cost of a main course at dinner or, if dinner is not served, at lunch; taxes and service charges are generally included.

GEORGE TOWN AND ENVIRONS

You'll find a fair number of restaurants in George Town, including such standbys as Guy Harvey's and Casanova, not to mention the splurge-worthy Grand Old House.

★ Fodor'sChoice ✕ **The Brasserie.** *Eclectic.* Actuaries, bankers,
$$$$ and CEOs frequent this contemporary throwback to a colonial country club for lunch and "attitude adjustment" happy hours for creative cocktails and complimentary canapés. Inviting fusion sea-to-table cuisine, emphasizing local ingredients whenever possible (the restaurant has its own boat and garden), includes terrific bar tapas. **Known for:** locavore's delight; creative small plates; power-broker hangout. ⑤ *Average main: $31* ⊠ *171 Elgin Ave., Cricket Sq., George Town* ☎ *345/945–1815* ⊕ *www.brasseriecayman.com* ⊘ *Closed weekends.*

FREE LOADING UP. Competition is fierce between Grand Cayman's many bars and restaurants. In addition to entertainment (from fish feeding to fire eating), even upscale joints host happy hours offering free hors d'oeuvres and/or drinks.

$$$ ✕ **Casanova Restaurant by the Sea.** *Italian.* Owner Tony Crescente and younger brother, maitre d' Carlo, offer a simpatico dining experience, practically exhorting you to *mangia* and sending you off with a chorus of ciaos. There's some decorative *formaggio* (cheese): murals of grape clusters and cavorting cherubs, paintings of the Amalfi Coast, and *una finestra sul mare* ("window to the sea") stenciled redundantly over arches opening onto the harbor. **Known for:** sensational harbor views; simpatico service; particularly fine sauces. ⑤ *Average main: $30* ⊠ *65 N. Church St., George Town* ☎ *345/949–7633* ⊕ *www.casanova.ky.*

$$$ ✕ **Da Fish Shack.** *Seafood.* This classic clapboard seaside shanty couldn't be homier: constructed from an old fishing vessel, the structure is an authentic representation of

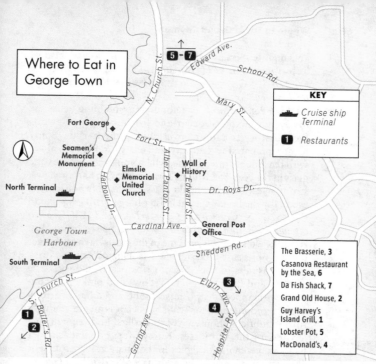

Where to Eat in George Town

original Caymanian architecture. The deck couldn't be better placed to savor the breezes and water views, and the chill Caribbean vibe makes it feel as if you're dining at a friend's home. **Known for:** terrific harbor views; delectable fish tacos; mellow ambience. ⑤ *Average main: $25* ⊠ *127 N. Church St., George Town* ☎ *345/947–8126* ⊕ *www. dafishshack.com.*

★ **Fodor'sChoice** ✕ **Grand Old House.** *European.* Built in 1908 **$$$$** as the Petra Plantation House and transformed into the island's first upscale establishment decades ago, this grande dame evokes bygone grandeur sans pretension. The interior rooms, awash in crystal, recall its plantation-house origins. **Known for:** elegant historic setting; comparatively affordable waterside tapas bar; classic continental fare with island twists. ⑤ *Average main: $47* ⊠ *648 S. Church St., George Town* ☎ *345/949–9333* ⊕ *www.grandoldhouse.com* ☾ *Closed Sept. and Sun. in low season. No lunch weekends.*

$$$$ ✕ **Guy Harvey's Island Grill.** *Seafood.* Guy Harvey's is a stylish upstairs bistro, with a mahogany furnishings, ship's lanterns, porthole windows, fishing rods, and Harvey's action-packed marine art. The cool blues echo the sea and sky on display from the balcony. **Known for:** affordable nightly specials; terrific tapas; luscious lobster bisque. Ⓢ *Average main: $38* ✉ *Aquaworld Duty-Free Mall, 55 S. Church St., George Town* ☎ *345/946–9000* ⊕ *www.guy-harveysgrill.com.*

$$$$ ✕ **Lobster Pot.** *Seafood.* The nondescript building belies the lovely marine-motif decor and luscious seafood at this second-story restaurant overlooking the harbor. Enjoy lobster prepared several ways (all à la sticker shock) along with reasonably priced wine, which you can sample by the glass in the cozy bar. **Known for:** scintillating harbor views; strong selection wines by the glass; predictably fine lobster, especially the Friday special lobster burger. Ⓢ *Average main: $50* ✉ *245 N. Church St., George Town* ☎ *345/949–2736* ⊕ *www.lobsterpot.ky* ⊗ *No lunch Sun. in off-season and Sat.*

$ ✕ **MacDonald's.** *Caribbean.* One of the locals' favorite burger joints—not a fast-food outlet—MacDonald's does a brisk lunch business in stick-to-your ribs basics like rotisserie chicken and fish escoveitch. Yellows and pinks predominate, with appetizing posters of food and a large cartoon chicken mounted on the wall; but decor is an afterthought to the politicos, housewives in curlers, and cops flirting shyly with the waitresses. **Known for:** popular islander hangout; perennial local pick for best burger; juicy rotisserie chicken. Ⓢ *Average main: $11* ✉ *99 Shedden Rd., George Town* ☎ *345/949–4640.*

SEVEN MILE BEACH

The lion's share of Grand Cayman restaurants is to be found along Seven Mile Beach, where most of the island's resorts are also located. Some are in the strip malls on the east side of West Bay Road, but many are in the resorts themselves.

★ Fodor$Choice ✕ **Abacus.** *Eclectic.* This handsome Camana Bay **$$$$** hangout, once more notable for its stunning decor (witness the smoked glass-and-cast-iron chandeliers) has been transformed into a foodie mecca by executive chef Will O'Hara. Credit his farm-to-table "contemporary Caribbean cuisine" and the solid relationships he's developed with local purveyors, farmers, and fishermen. **Known for:** fab farm-to-table menu; sophisticated space; pork belly specials a standout. Ⓢ *Average main: $36* ✉ *45 Market St., Camana Bay* ☎ *345/623–8282* ⊕ *www.abacus.ky* ⊗ *Closed Sun.*

★ Fodor$Choice ✕ **Agua.** *Italian.* This quietly hip spot plays **$$$$** up an aquatic theme with indigo glass fixtures, black-and-white photos of bridges and waterfalls, and cobalt-and-white walls subtly recalling foamy waves. Its young,

CLOSE UP

Farm Fresh

A joint initiative of the Cayman Islands Agricultural Society, the Ministry of Agriculture, the Department of Agriculture, and local vendors-purveyors, the **Market at the Grounds** is a jambalaya of sights, sounds, and smells held every Saturday from 7 am at the Stacy Watler Agricultural Pavilion in Lower Valley (East End). Local growers, fishers, home gardeners and chefs (dispensing scrumptious, cheap cuisine), and artisans display their wares in a tranquil green setting. To preserve Caymanian flavor, everything must be 100% locally grown. Participating craftspeople and artists, from couturiers to musicians, must use local designs and materials whenever possible. The market fosters a renewed spirit of community, providing literal feedback into the production process, while the interaction with visitors promotes understanding of island culture.

international chefs emphasize seafood, preparing regional dishes from around the globe with a Caymanian slant, albeit emphasizing Peruvian and Italian specialties from *tiraditos* to *tiramisu*. **Known for:** sensational service; winning wine list and creative cocktails; superlative ceviches. ⑤ *Average main: $39 ⊠ Galleria Plaza, Seven Mile Beach* ☎ *345/949–2482 ⊕ www.agua.ky.*

$ ✕ **Al La Kebab.** *Middle Eastern.* The Silvermans started by serving late-night kebabs and gyros. Today their eatery works miracles out of two makeshift lean-tos splashed in vibrant colors and is still open until 4 am weeknights, 2 am weekends. **Known for:** fun late-night hangout; impressive variety of sauces; bargain prices. ⑤ *Average main: $12 ⊠ Marquee Plaza, West Bay Rd., Seven Mile Beach* ☎ *345/943–4343 ⊕ www.kebab.ky.*

★ Fodor'sChoice ✕ **Bàcaro.** *Italian.* Bàcaro (likely derived from
$$$ Bacchus, Roman god of wine) is the Venetian slang term for a gastropub, dispensing upscale versions of downhome *cichetti* (the city's beloved take on tapas). This dazzling yacht club eatery, boasting gorgeous views of the marina and modish decor (terrific terrace, wonderful black-and-white fishing photos, ropes hung from the ceiling to suggest both keels and sails), delivers on the name's promise thanks to the artistry of Venetian-born head chef–owner Federico Destro, late of Luca. **Known for:** fabulous small plates; comparatively inexpensive and superb tasting menu; refined yet chill atmosphere. ⑤ *Average main: $30 ⊠ Cayman Islands Yacht Club, Yacht Drive,*

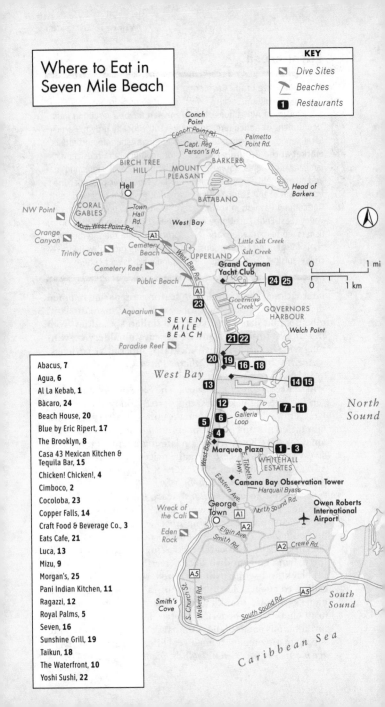

Where to Eat in Seven Mile Beach

KEY
- Dive Sites
- Beaches
- 1 Restaurants

Abacus, **7**

Agua, **6**

Al La Kebab, **1**

Bàcaro, **24**

Beach House, **20**

Blue by Eric Ripert, **17**

The Brooklyn, **8**

Casa 43 Mexican Kitchen & Tequila Bar, **15**

Chicken! Chicken!, **4**

Cimboco, **2**

Cocoloba, **23**

Copper Falls, **14**

Craft Food & Beverage Co., **3**

Eats Cafe, **21**

Luca, **13**

Mizu, **9**

Morgan's, **25**

Pani Indian Kitchen, **11**

Ragazzi, **12**

Royal Palms, **5**

Seven, **16**

Sunshine Grill, **19**

Taikun, **18**

The Waterfront, **10**

Yoshi Sushi, **22**

Governor's Creek, Seven Mile Beach ☎ 345/749–4800 ⊕ *www.bacaro.ky* ⊗ *Closed Mon.*

$$$$ ✕ **Beach House** (*Casa Havana*). *Seafood.* This refined eatery glamorously channels South Beach and Santa Monica, with a sexy black bar, an earthy color scheme, and sparkly ecru curtains dividing dining spaces. Executive chef Sandy Tuason apprenticed with such masters as the Roux brothers, Daniel Boulud, and David Burke. **Known for:** superb seafood, especially the charcuterie and salt-baked fish; well-considered if pricey wine list; elegant yet unstuffy atmosphere. ⑤ *Average main: $40* ⊠ *Westin Grand Cayman Seven Mile Beach Resort & Spa, West Bay Rd., Seven Mile Beach* ☎ 345/945–3800 ⊕ *www.westingrandcayman.com* ⊗ *No lunch.*

★ **Fodor'sChoice** ✕ **Blue by Eric Ripert.** *Seafood.* *Top Chef* judge **$$$$** Eric Ripert's trademark ethereal seafood (executed by his handpicked brigade), flawless but not fawning service, swish setting, and soothing, unpretentious sophistication make this one of the Caribbean's finest restaurants. Choose from hedonistic six- and seven-course tasting menus (with or without wine pairing); there are also trendy "almost raw" and "barely touched" options. **Known for:** stratospheric prices but worth it; stellar service; brilliant modern French recipes and local ingredients. ⑤ *Average main: $150* ⊠ *Ritz-Carlton Grand Cayman, West Bay Rd., Seven Mile Beach* ☎ 345/943–9000 ⊕ *www.ritzcarlton.com* ⊗ *Closed Sun. and Mon. and Sept.–mid-Nov. No lunch.*

$$$ ✕ **The Brooklyn.** *Eclectic.* The industrial chic setting of this **FAMILY** wildly popular pizza and pasta joint cleverly recalls similar Brooklyn eateries in DUMBO and Williamsburg with natural wood tables for family-style dining, exposed piping, oversize metal lighting fixtures, distressed floors, and silkscreen paintings of musicians like Ray Charles and Diana Ross in Fauvist tones. The food proves equally trendy and appealing. **Known for:** creative pizzas; buzzy atmosphere; smashing cocktails. ⑤ *Average main: $26* ⊠ *The Crescent, Camana Bay* ☎ 345/640–0005 ⊕ *www. thebrooklyncayman.com.*

★ **Fodor'sChoice** ✕ **Casa 43 Mexican Kitchen & Tequila Bar.** *Mexican.* **$$** Mariachi music, sombreros, and intricate Talavera tile work set the tone at this authentic and innovative Mexican eatery tucked away off West Bay Road. Start with the savory ceviches (winners include Caribbean shrimp, Peruvian-style red snapper, and tuna Chino-Latino in soy with sesame, chile, mint, and cilantro). **Known for:** fun, festive staff and atmosphere; tasty tacos and chilaquiles; marvelous margaritas. ⑤ *Average main: $20* ⊠ *43 Canal Point Dr., Seven Mile*

Blue by Eric Ripert

Beach ⊕ Behind Copper Falls Steakhouse ☎ *345/949–4343*
⊕ *www.casa43.ky* ☉ *Closed Sun.*

$ × **Chicken! Chicken!** *Caribbean.* Devotees would probably
FAMILY award four exclamation points to the marvelously moist
chicken, slow-roasted on a hardwood open-hearth rotis-
serie. Most customers grab takeout, but the decor is appealing for a fast-food joint; the clever interior replicates an
old-time Cayman cottage. **Known for:** chicken, chicken,
and chicken; fantastic side dishes; low low prices. ⑤ *Average
main: $12* ⊠ *West Shore Centre, West Bay Rd., Seven Mile
Beach* ☎ *345/945–2290* ⊕ *www.chicken2.com.*

$$ × **Cimboco.** *Eclectic.* This animated space celebrates all
things fun and Caribbean with walls saturated in orange,
lemon, and lavender; cobalt glass fixtures; and flames
dancing up the exhibition kitchen's huge wood-burning
oven. The *Cimboco* was the first motorized sailing ship
built in Cayman (in 1927) and for 20 years the lifeline
to the outside world; National Archive photographs and
old newspapers invest the space with still more character.
Known for: fun, boldly colored decor; fair prices and hefty
servings; clever riffs on staples like pizza with local ingre-
dients. ⑤ *Average main: $19* ⊠ *Marquee Plaza, West Bay
Rd. at Harquail Bypass, Seven Mile Beach* ☎ *345/947–2782*
⊕ *www.cimboco.com.*

★ **Fodor's**Choice × **Coccoloba.** *Mexican Fusion.* Despite the decep-
$$$ tively chill vibe, open-air setup replete with thatching and
colorful hand-painted tiles and plates, the fare is haute

south-of-the-border. You won't sample finer *chicharrones* (in tangy tequila barbecue sauce), fish tacos, or *elote* (corn off the cob with cotija cheese, cilantro, lime, and chipotle aioli) outside the Yucatan, while the intensely flavored flat-iron steak with mole jus and chimichurri might make even dedicated vegetarians think twice. **Known for:** killer sunset views; innovative Mexican cuisine; knowledgeable friendly bartenders. ⑤ *Average main: $26* ✉ *Kimpton Seafire Resort & Spa, 60 Tanager Way, Seven Mile Beach* ☎ *345/746–0000, 345/746–4111* ⊕ *www.seafireresortandspa.com, www.coccolobacaymanislands.com.*

$$$$ ✕ **Copper Falls.** *Steakhouse.* The restaurant's tag line, "A Rare Steakhouse, Very Well Done," is only a touch hyperbolic. The brashly contemporary look (copper-clad waterfalls and hand-painted metal bas relief contrasting with century-old Douglas fir wainscoting and high-back suede booths) screams corporate takeover in progress. **Known for:** clubby soigne ambience; mouthwatering steaks; nice extras. ⑤ *Average main: $56* ✉ *43 Canal Point Rd., The Strand, Seven Mile Beach* ☎ *345/945–4755* ⊕ *www.copperfallssteakhouse.com* ☾ *Closed Mon. Sept.–Oct. No lunch.*

★ Fodor'sChoice ✕ **Craft Food & Beverage Co.** *Eclectic.* Arguably Cayman's first true gastropub, Craft impresses with gorgeous postindustrial decor (contrasting warm white exposed brick with gray piping) and contemporary rustic cuisine that defies labels. The kitchen dubs it "familiar food with a twist." The globe-trotting menu changes monthly and the executive chef takes sabbaticals, traveling the world for inspiration. **Known for:** hip but not tragically trendy; awesome cocktail and beer selection; great nightly specials. ⑤ *Average main: $27* ✉ *Marquee Plaza, West Bay Rd., Seven Mile Beach* ⊹ *Across from the Marriott* ☎ *345/640–0004* ⊕ *www.craftcayman.com.*

$$$

$$$ ✕ **Eats Cafe.** *Eclectic.* This busy and eclectic eatery has a FAMILY vast menu (Cajun to Chinese), including smashing breakfasts. The decor is dramatic—crimson booths and walls, flat-screen TVs lining the counter, steel pendant lamps, an exhibition kitchen, gigantic flower paintings, and Andy Warhol reproductions. **Known for:** fun buzzy vibe; reasonable prices; extensive "Greek diner" one-from-column-A menu. ⑤ *Average main: $24* ✉ *Falls Plaza, West Bay Rd., Seven Mile Beach* ☎ *345/943–3287* ⊕ *www.eats.ky.*

★ Fodor'sChoice ✕ **Luca.** *Italian.* Owners Paolo Polloni and Andi Marcher spared no expense in creating a smart beachfront trattoria that wouldn't be out of place in L.A. Everything was handpicked: wine wall of more than 3,000 international

$$$$

bottles; Murano glass fixtures; arty blown-up photographs; leather banquettes; and a curving onyx-top bar. **Known for:** sophisticated decor; lovely pastas; fabulous if expensive wine list. ⑤ *Average main: $42* ⊠ *Caribbean Club, 871 West Bay Rd., Seven Mile Beach* ☎ *345/623–4550* ⊕ *luca.ky* ⊘ *Closed Mon. in Sept. and Oct. No lunch Sat.*

★ FodorsChoice ✕ **Mizu.** *Asian.* The decor, courtesy of Hong
$$ Kong designer Kitty Chan, is as sensuous as a 21st-century opium den with a back-lit dragon, contemporary Buddhas, glowing granite bar, wildly hued throw pillows, and enormous mirrors. The last trots effortlessly all over Asia for culinary inspiration: terrific tuna tartare, decadent duck gyoza, killer kung pao chicken, smashing Singapore fried noodles, heavenly honey-glazed ribs, beautifully crispy Okinawan-style pork belly, and two dozen ultrafresh maki (try the signature roll). **Known for:** ultrahip decor and staff; huge portions ideal for sharing; surprisingly authentic Asian fare. ⑤ *Average main: $20* ⊠ *Camana Bay* ☎ *345/640–0001* ⊕ *www.mizucayman.com.*

★ FodorsChoice ✕ **Morgan's.** *Eclectic.* Energetic, effervescent
$$$ Janie Schweiger patrols the front while husband Richard rules the kitchen at this simpatico marina spot with smashing Governor's Creek views. Locals and fishermen literally cruise into the adjacent dock for refueling of all sorts. **Known for:** delightful husband-wife owners; fun peripatetic menu; glorious patio seating overlooking the marina. ⑤ *Average main: $29* ⊠ *Governor's Creek, Cayman Islands Yacht Club, Seven Mile Beach* ☎ *345/946–7049* ⊕ *www. morganscayman.com* ⊘ *Closed Tues. and Oct.*

★ FodorsChoice ✕ **Pani Indian Kitchen.** *Indian.* In every respect from
$$$ the decor to the cuisine, Pani is a joyous celebration of street food from around the subcontinent, with an haute gloss. The space breathtakingly creates an Indian street bazaar indoors: bamboo-and-burlap awnings, billowing multihue fabric, representations of such deities as Ganesha, a wall of dyed tea bags, and huge brass tandoori urns in the open kitchen. **Known for:** wonderfully flavorful options for vegetarians; fantastic bargain lunch menu; delightful decor including an entire wall of dyed tea bags. ⑤ *Average main: $21* ⊠ *The Crescent, Camana Bay* ☎ *345/640–0007* ⊕ *www.panicayman.com.*

★ FodorsChoice ✕ **Ragazzi.** *Italian.* The name means "good bud-
$$$ dies," and this strip-mall jewel percolates with conversation
FAMILY and good strong espresso. The airy space is convivial: blond woods, periwinkle walls and columns, and handsome artworks of beach scenes, sailboats, and palm trees. **Known for:** reasonable prices by Cayman standards; scrumptious authentic piz-

zas and pastas; thoughtful wine list showcasing lesser-known regions. ⑤ *Average main: $25* ⊠ *Buckingham Square, West Bay Rd., Seven Mile Beach* ☎ *345/945–3484* ⊕ *www.ragazzi.ky.*

$$$$ ✕**Royal Palms.** *Eclectic.* This class act appeals to a casual, suave crowd, many of them regulars, who appreciate its consistent quality, efficient service, soothing seaside setting, top-notch entertainment, and surprisingly reasonable prices. The space is cannily divided into four areas, each with its own look and feel, including private beach cabanas (no extra charge). **Known for:** clever variations on Mediterranean standards; wildly popular evening entertainment; sensational seaside setting. ⑤ *Average main: $31* ⊠ *537 West Bay Rd., Seven Mile Beach* ☎ *345/945–6358* ⊕ *www. reefgrill.com* ⊘ *No dinner Sun. May–Nov.*

★ **Fodor's**Choice ✕**Seven.** *Steakhouse.* The Ritz-Carlton's all-purpose dining room transforms from a bustling breakfast buffet to an elegant evening eatery. Tall potted palms, soaring ceilings, a black-and-beige color scheme, twin wine walls bracketing a trendy family-style table, and the tiered pool outside are lighted to stylish effect. **Known for:** magnificent steaks; creative sides like lobster-twice-baked mashed potatoes; terrific happy hour cocktail and bar bite bargains. ⑤ *Average main: $51* ⊠ *Ritz-Carlton Grand Cayman, West Bay Rd., Seven Mile Beach* ☎ *345/943–9000* ⊕ *www.ritzcarlton.com.*

$$$ ✕**Sunshine Grill.** *Caribbean.* This cheerful, cherished locals' **FAMILY** secret serves haute comfort food at bargain prices. Even the chattel-style poolside building, painted a delectable lemon with lime shutters, multihued interior columns, and orange and blueberry accents, whets the appetite. **Known for:** warm family-friendly atmosphere and staff; fantastic affordable dinner specials; one of locals' top choices for burgers. ⑤ *Average main: $23* ⊠ *Sunshine Suites Resort, 1465 Esterley Tibbetts Hwy., Seven Mile Beach* ☎ *345/949–3000, 345/946–5848* ⊕ *www.sunshinesuites.com.*

★ **Fodor's**Choice ✕**Taikun.** *Japanese.* Taikun is an archaic Japa- **$$$** nese term of esteem, loosely translated as "Supreme Com- **FAMILY** mander." It's an appropriate designation for this sensuous sushi spot, clad in black with crimson and gray accents and dominated by a buzzy communal table. Start with one of the terrific cocktails or indulge in the superlative sake flights, which can be optimally paired with your sushi. **Known for:** simply sensational sushi; attention to detail include grinding wasabi at table; refined yet relaxed ambience. ⑤ *Average main: $30* ⊠ *Ritz-Carlton Grand Cayman, West Bay Rd., Seven Mile Beach* ☎ *345/943–9000* ⊕ *www. ritzcarlton.com/GrandCayman.*

3

$$ ✕The Waterfront. *Diner.* Ultracontemporary design with
FAMILY industrial elements (exposed piping, raw timber, tugboat
salvage) is a counterpoint to the down-home fare at this
bustling glorified diner, whose choice seats are on the patio.
Comfort food aficionados can launch into the splendid
chicken and waffles, meat loaf, and poutine. **Known for:**
fantastic comfort food like poutine and a killer cinnamon
roll; fun for families; pleasant outdoor seating area. Ⓢ *Average main: $19* ⊠ *The Crescent, Camana Bay* ☎ *345/640–
0002* ⊕ *www.waterfrontcayman.com.*

$$$ ✕Yoshi Sushi. *Japanese.* This modish locals' lair serves
superlative sushi. The main room's scarlet cushions, cherry
blown-glass pendant lamps, leather-and-bamboo accents,
orchids, and maroon walls create a sensuous, charged vibe.
Known for: innovative rolls and sushi "pizzas"; excellent
cocktails; cool vibe. Ⓢ *Average main: $23* ⊠ *Falls Plaza,
West Bay Rd., Seven Mile Beach* ☎ *345/943–9674* ⊕ *www.
eats.ky/yoshisushi.*

WEST BAY

There are fewer restaurant choices in West Bay, but there
are some spots that are worth the trip. Be sure to have
good driving directions when heading out into this area.

$$$$ ✕Calypso Grill. *Eclectic.* Shack-chic describes this inviting
split-level eatery, splashed in Dr. Seuss primary colors, with
hardwood furnishings, terra-cotta floors, trompe l'oeil shutters,
and (real) French doors opening onto sweeping North Sound
vistas. If the interior is like a Caribbean painting, the outdoor
deck, with a view of frigate birds circling fishing boats, is a
Winslow Homer. **Known for:** wonderfully colorful decor;
entrancing views of North Sound; superb seafood. Ⓢ *Average
main: $44* ⊠ *Morgan's Harbour, West Bay* ☎ *345/949–3948*
⊕ *www.calypsogrillcayman.com* ⊙ *Closed Mon.*

★ **Fodor's**Choice ✕**Catch.** *Seafood.* With the fishermen practi-
$$$$ cally cruising up to your table with glistening seafood, this
restaurant right on the harbor lives up to its name. Even
the decor is appetizing, with walls daubed in edible hues
like mustard, tomato, and mint, setting off bleached dis-
tressed wood. **Known for:** gorgeous harbour views ; sterling
wine and cocktail lists; fabulous brunch tapas. Ⓢ *Average
main: $40* ⊠ *Batabano Rd., Morgan's Harbour, West Bay*
☎ *345/949–4321* ⊕ *www.catch.ky.*

$$$$ ✕Cracked Conch. *Eclectic.* This island institution effort-
lessly blends upscale and down-home. The interior gleams
from the elaborate light-and-water sculpture at the gor-

CLOSE UP

Culinary Quality Control

In more than a decade at the helm of New York's Le Bernardin, sometime *Top Chef* panelist Eric Ripert has garnered every gastronomic accolade. Born in Antibes on the French Riviera, Ripert apprenticed at Parisian institution La Tour d'Argent and Joël Robuchon's Jamin, then worked stateside with Jean-Louis Palladin and David Bouley before Le Bernardin reeled him in. He opened his first "name" restaurant, Blue by Eric Ripert, at the Ritz-Carlton Grand Cayman in 2005. Others have since followed.

The Caribbean wasn't on Ripert's radar, as he has told us, but "the resort owner, Michael Ryan, was in New York for dinner at Le Bernardin. He wanted to discuss the Ritz and me opening its signature restaurant. When I came down, he picked me up, put me on a boat to swim at Stingray City, loaded me with champagne, then came straight here to discuss business. ... I loved it, felt confident because of his commitment to quality and service."

The greatest challenge was "the quality of the seafood, which sounds illogical, but most fish here comes frozen from the United States. We visited fishermen, created a network, to get fresh catch regularly. It's the only item the hotel allows cash for, so [executive chef Frederic Morineau]

carries a big wad! We fought passionately for the quality of the seafood, since that's one of my trademarks. And with so few farmers and growers on island ... produce was even more challenging, but we found squash, salad greens, herbs."

"Trying to use what's already here inspires me," says Morineau. "It's cooking in the landscape. I can now get lemongrass, thyme, mint, basil, papaya, mango, callaloo, sweet potatoes, good stew tomatoes, Scotch bonnet, and other peppers. I'm a big advocate of the locally produced Cayman sea salt." He encourages local purveyors, but paramount was persuading management to commit the funds for specialty products worth the price. "We work with a couple of commercial fishing boats that bring huge wahoo, ocean yellowtail, deep-water snapper from as far afield as Mexico. So fresh and so beautiful, a pleasure to work with."

Ripert draws parallels to his Mediterranean upbringing. "It's a different feel and look, of course, as are the cooking ingredients and preparations. But both cultures place great emphasis on food as a key part of their lives and borrow from many heritages. And both cultures know how to relax and enjoy themselves!"

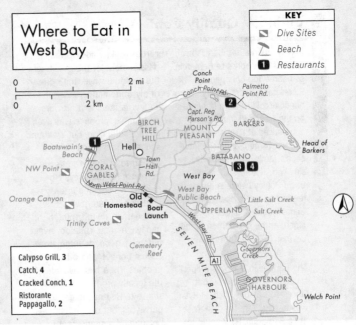

Where to Eat in West Bay

Conch Point

Palmetto Point Rd.

Conch Point Rd.

Capt. Reg Parson's Rd.

BARKERS

BIRCH TREE HILL

MOUNT PLEASANT

Head of Barkers

Boatswain's Beach

Hell

BATABANO

NW Point

CORAL GABLES

Town Hall Rd.

West Bay

Orange Canyon

North West Point Rd.

West Bay Public Beach

Little Salt Creek

Salt Creek

Old Homestead

Boat Launch

UPPERLAND

Trinity Caves

Cemetery Reef

SEVEN MILE BEACH

Governors Creek

GOVERNORS HARBOUR

Welch Point

Calypso Grill, **3**
Catch, **4**
Cracked Conch, **1**
Ristorante Pappagallo, **2**

geous mosaic-and-mahogany entrance Bubble Bar to the plush booths with subtly embedded lighting. **Known for:** sensational views; creative dishes fusing local ingredients and Continental classics; lively waterside bar section with specials. $ *Average main: $45* ⊠ *857 Northwest Point Rd., West Bay* ☎ *345/945–5217* ⊕ *www.crackedconch.com.ky* ⊘ *Closed Sept.–mid-Oct. No lunch June–Aug.*

$$$$ ✕ **Ristorante Pappagallo.** *Italian.* Pappagallo, Italian for "parrot," hauntingly perches on the edge of a lagoon in a 14-acre bird sanctuary. Inside, riotously colored macaws, cockatoos, and parrots perch on swings behind plate glass, primping, preening, and practically commenting on the billing and cooing clientele. **Known for:** marvelously romantic "jungle" setting; delectable Italian fare such as osso buco; smart food and wine/cocktail pairings. $ *Average main: $38* ⊠ *Barkers, 444B Conch Point Rd., West Bay* ☎ *345/949–1119* ⊕ *www.pappagallo.ky* ⊘ *No lunch.*

EAST END

While it can be at least a half-hour drive out here, some of the restaurants in East End are worth the trip from George Town.

CLOSE UP

Food Fêtes

Gastronomy is big business on Grand Cayman, as upmarket eateries bank on the tourist dollar. Increasingly popular culinary events introduce visitors to local culture while beefing up biz, especially off-season. Celeb chef Eric Ripert debuted "Caribbean Rundown" weekend in 2007 at his Blue by Eric Ripert in the Ritz-Carlton, including cooking classes, fishing trips, and gala dinners, *Top Chef* competitor Dale Levitzki in tow.

It was such a success that *Food & Wine* cosponsors the subsequent editions—now called Cayman Cookout—every January, with even more top toques stirring the broth: a recipe for success in this case. Both fests benefit local charities. February's "A Taste of Cayman" has titillated taste buds for more than two decades, thanks to more than 30 participating restaurants, raffles, entertainment, and cook-offs.

$$$$ ✕**The Lighthouse.** *Seafood.* This lighthouse surrounded by
FAMILY fluttering flags serves as a beacon for hungry East End explorers. The interior replicates a yacht: polished hardwood floors, ship's lanterns, mosaic hurricane lamps, steering wheels, portholes, and waiters in crew's garb with chevrons. **Known for:** marvelous sea views; affordably priced specials; cooking classes. ⓈＡverage main: $36 ✉2114 Bodden Town Rd., Oceanside, Breakers, East End ☎345/947–2047 ⊕www.lighthouse.ky ☉ Closed Mon.

$$ ✕**Vivine's Kitchen.** *Caribbean.* Cars practically block the road at this unprepossessing hot spot for classic Caymanian food—literally Vivine and Ray Watler's home. Prime seating is in the waterfront courtyard, serenaded by rustling sea grape leaves, crashing surf, and screeching gulls. **Known for:** authentic Caymanian food; typical island hospitality; good prices for giant portions. ⓈＡverage main: $17 ✉Austin Dr., Gun Bay, East End ☎345/947–7435 ▭No credit cards.

NORTH SIDE

The North Side has few good places to eat, but two spots stand out.

$$ ✕**Kaibo Beach Bar and Grill.** *Caribbean.* Overlooking the North Sound, this beach hangout rocks days (fantastic lunches that cost half the price of dinner, festive atmosphere including impromptu volleyball tourneys, and free Wi-Fi) and serves murderous margaritas and mudslides well into the evening to boisterous yachties, locals, sports buffs, and

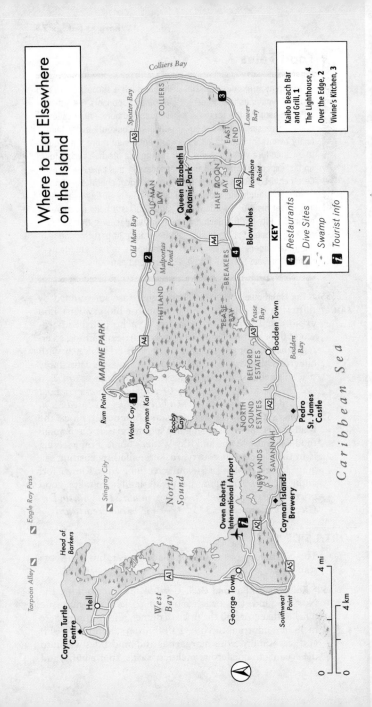

Where to Eat Elsewhere on the Island

Kaibo Beach Bar and Grill, 1
The Lighthouse, 4
Over the Edge, 2
Vivine's Kitchen, 3

KEY

4 Restaurants
Dive Sites
Swamp
i Tourist info

Colliers Bay

Spotter Bay

COLLIERS

Lower Bay

EAST END

Old Man Bay

OLD MAN BAY

Queen Elizabeth II Botanic Park

HALF MOON BAY

Ironshore Point

Malportas Pond

HUTLAND

BREAKERS

Blowholes

PEASE BAY

MARINE PARK

A4

Pease Bay

A3

Rum Point

Water Cay

Cayman Kai

BELFORD ESTATES

Bodden Town

Bodden Bay

Booby Cay

NORTH SOUND ESTATES

A2

Pedro St. James Castle

Stingray City

North Sound

SAVANNAH

NEWLANDS

Cayman Islands Brewery

Head of Barkers

Owen Roberts International Airport

A2

A5

Tarpoon Alley

Eagle Ray Pass

Cayman Turtle Centre

Hell

A1

West Bay

George Town

Southwest Point

Caribbean Sea

4 mi

4 km

0

0

CLOSE UP

Eating at a Home Kitchen

Aspiring Anthony Bourdains on Grand Cayman should seek out roadside vans, huts, kiosks, and stalls dishing out unfamiliar grub. These casual spots offer authentic fare at very fair prices, with main dishes and heaping helpings of sides costing under CI$10. If you thought Mickey D's special sauce or Coke was a secret formula, try prying prized recipes handed down for generations from these islanders.

Rankin's Jerk Centre. A faux cow and pig greet you at Rankin's Jerk Centre, where you can savor Miss Rankin's scrumptious turtle stew and jerk dishes in her alluring garden. ✉ 3032 Shamrock Rd., Bodden Town, Grand Cayman ☎ 345/947–3155.

Captain Herman's Fish Fry. You can't miss the vibrant marine life mural and key lime-colored walls topped by a roof adorned with conch shells at this seaside spot beloved for sweet-and-sour shrimp, oxtail and beans, conch chowder, and more. ✉ Sea View Rd. off Indiana Lane, East End, Grand Cayman ☎ 345/924–4007.

Chester's Fish Fry. Chester's Fish Fry has a devoted following for his jerk pork, fried fish, and downy fritters. ✉ 563 Bodden Town Rd., Bodden Town, Grand Cayman ☎ 345/939–3474.

Two of these most casual eateries on the island are George Town institutions.

Tony's Jerk Foods. Even politicos stand in line at Tony's Jerk Foods, which serves everything from cow foot to conch stew (you can't miss the exterior's beach mural). ✉ 193 School Rd., George Town, Grand Cayman ☎ 345/916–6860.

Heritage Kitchen. West Bay's popular family-run Heritage Kitchen serves up legendary raconteur Tunny Powell's fish tea, barbecue ribs, and fish fry—with a generous portion of local lore. It's only open sporadically, so look for it when you're in the area. ✉ Just off Boggy Sand Rd., West Bay, Grand Cayman.

expats. Enjoy New England–style conch chowder with a hint of heat, smoked mahimahi pâté, hefty burgers, and wondrous wraps, either on the multitiered deck garlanded with ships' rope and Christmas lights or in hammocks and thatched cabanas amid the palms. **Known for:** boisterous crowd; fun beach events; top-notch pub grub. ⑤ *Average main: $19* ✉ *585 Water Cay Rd., Rum Point* ☎ *345/947–9975* ⊕ *www.kaibo.ky.*

$$$ ✕**Over the Edge.** *Caribbean.* This fun, funky seaside spot brims with character and characters. (A soused regular might welcome you by reciting "the daily lunch special: chilled barley soup … That's beer.") The nutty nautical decor—brass ships' lanterns dangle from the ceiling, and steering wheels, lacquered turtle shells, and fishing photos adorn the walls—contrasts with cool mirrored ads for Gitanes and Mumm Cordon Rouge and the trendily semi-open kitchen with fresh fish prominently displayed. **Known for:** delectable local fare; island insiders' hangout; appealing semi-enclosed patio. Ⓢ *Average main: $21* ⊠ *312 North Side Rd., Old Man Bay* ☎ *345/947–9568.*

WHERE TO STAY IN
GRAND CAYMAN

Updated
by Jordan
Simon

DESPITE ITS SMALL SIZE, GRAND Cayman offers a surprising range of accommodations: large luxury resorts, medium-size chain hotels, cozy condo enclaves, locally owned guesthouses—from boutique-y to budget, not to mention private villas.

The massive Ritz-Carlton resort on Seven Mile Beach was the first of several larger developments constructed under new laws allowing seven-story buildings. It was followed by the classy Caribbean Club Condominiums and the rebuilt upscale Beachcomber. Now high-rises sprout like fungi along Seven Mile Beach, each vowing and vying to be better—or at least grander—than the last. Then the zoning restrictions changed once again to permit the even higher-rise Kimpton Seafire, completed in 2016.

Some of the acceptance of ever-grander development can be attributed to the lingering devastation of 2004's Hurricane Ivan, which totaled the island; evidence of its fury still lingers. The 230-room Hyatt Regency hotel, long the island standard-bearer, never recovered from the damage; Hyatt eventually withdrew from its last management responsibilities. For good or bad, Ivan provided many complexes with an excuse to renovate, even rebuild from the ground up and go ever higher. Although the tacky, dilapidated condo enclaves were swept away, now practically every sizable lot of Seven Mile Beach is in various stages of development.

Brace yourself for resort prices—there are few accommodations in the lower-cost ranges in Grand Cayman. You'll also find no big all-inclusive resorts on Grand Cayman, and very few offer a meal plan of any kind. Happily, parking is always free at island hotels and resorts.

WHERE TO STAY

Seven Mile Beach is Boardwalk and Park Place for most vacationers. In a quirk of development, however, most of the hotels sit across the street from the beach (though they usually have beach clubs, bars, water-sports concessions, and other facilities directly on the sand). Most of Grand Cayman's condo resorts offer direct access to Grand Cayman's prime sandy real estate. Snorkelers should note that only the northern and southern ends of SMB feature spectacular reef development; the northern end is much

Buildings in George Town

quieter, so if you're looking for action, stay anywhere from the Westin Grand Cayman south, where all manner of restaurants and bars are walkable.

Tranquil **West Bay** retains the feel of an old-time fishing village; diving is magnificent in this area, but lodging options are limited, especially now that the long-promised Mandarin Oriental remains on indefinite hold.

Those who want to get away from it all should head to the bucolic **East End** and **North Side,** dotted with condo resorts and villas. The dive sites here are particularly pristine.

The **Cayman Kai/Rum Point,** starting at West Bay across the North Sound, offers the single largest concentration of villas and condo resorts, stressing barefoot elegance.

Hotel reviews have been shortened. For full information, visit Fodors.com.

WHAT IT COSTS IN U.S. DOLLARS				
	$	**$$**	**$$$**	**$$$$**
Hotels	under $275	$275–$375	$376–$475	over $475

Prices in the hotel reviews are the lowest cost of a standard double room in high season, excluding taxes, service charges, and meal plans (except at all-inclusives). Prices for rentals are the lowest per-night cost for a one-bedroom unit in high season.

HOTELS AND RESORTS

Grand Cayman offers something for every traveler, with well-known chain properties in every price range and style. Accommodations run the gamut from outrageously deluxe to all-suites to glorified motor lodges. Add to that locally run hostelries that often offer better bang for the buck. Still, in a Caymanian quirk, condo resorts take up most of the prime beach real estate. And, with a couple of exceptions, hotels along Seven Mile Beach actually sit across the road from the beach.

B&BS, INNS, AND GUESTHOUSES

They may be some distance from the beach and short on style and facilities, or they may be surprisingly elegant, but all these lodgings offer a friendly atmosphere, equally friendly prices, and your best shot at getting to know the locals. Rooms are clean and simple at the very least, and most have private baths.

CONDOMINIUMS AND PRIVATE VILLAS

On Grand Cayman the number of available condos and villas greatly outnumbers hotel rooms. Most condos are very similar, with telephones, satellite TV, air-conditioning, living and dining areas, patios, and parking. Differences are the quality of in-condo amenities, facilities within their individual complexes (though pools, hot tubs, and barbecue grills are usually standard), proximity to town and the beach, and views. Some condos are privately owned and rented out directly by the owners; other complexes are made up solely of short-term rentals.

Grand Cayman's private villa rentals range from cozy one-bedroom bungalows to grand five-bedroom manses. Some stand completely independent; others may be located in a larger complex or enclave. Although at first glance rental fees for villas may seem high, larger units can offer significant savings over hotels for families or couples traveling together. Few hotels on Grand Cayman are so moderately priced. And, as in a condo, a full kitchen helps reduce the stratospheric price of dining out; a laundry room helps with cleanup, especially for families. Unless otherwise noted, all villas have landline phones, and local calls are usually free; phones are generally locked for international calls, though Internet phone service could be included. Villa agents can usually help you rent a cell phone.

Rates are highest during the winter season from mid-December through mid-April. Most condo and villa rentals require a minimum stay, often five to seven nights in high season (during the Christmas holiday season the minimum will be at least one week and is sometimes two weeks, plus there are exorbitant fees). Off-season minimums are usually three to five nights.

Several of the condo- and villa-rental companies have websites where you can see pictures of the privately owned units and villas they represent; many properties are represented exclusively, others handled by several agents. In general, the farther north you go on Seven Mile Beach, the older and more affordable the property. Note also that many offices close on Sunday; if that's your date of arrival, they'll usually make arrangements for your arrival. There's often no maid service on Sunday either, as the island practically shuts down.

We no longer recommend individual private villas, especially since they frequently change agents. Nevertheless, among the properties we've inspected worth looking for are Coral Reef, Venezia, Villa Habana, Great Escapes, Fishbones, and Pease Bay House.

The **Cayman Islands Department of Tourism** (⊕ *www.caymanislands.ky*) provides a list of condominiums and small rental apartments. There are several condo and villa enclaves available on the beach, especially on the North Side near Cayman Kai, away from bustling Seven Mile Beach.

Quoted prices for villa and private condo rentals usually include government tax and often service fees (be sure to verify this). As a general rule of thumb, Seven Mile Beach properties receive daily maid service except on Sunday, but at villas and condos elsewhere on the island, extra services such as cleaning must be prearranged for an extra charge.

Cayman Island Vacations. Longtime Cayman homeowners Don and Linda Martin represent more than 50 villas and condos (including their own). Extremely helpful with island suggestions, they can make arrangements for a rental car, diving discounts, and extras, and Linda is a leading wedding coordinator. ☎ *813/854–1201, 888/208–8935* ⊕ *www.caymanvacation.com*.

★ Fodor's Choice **Cayman Villas.** Cayman Villas represents villas and condos on Grand Cayman and Little Cayman; from studios to six-bedrooms with private pool. They'll gladly facilitate connections with potential staff from chefs to

Caribbean Club

chauffeurs, recommend restaurants and tour operators, and even put you in touch with wedding coordinators. A great selling point: every property has a manager, available 24/7 via cell phone, who lives on-site or nearby. They work with industry leader WIMCO. ⊠ *177 Owen Roberts Dr., George Town* ☎ *800/235–5888, 345/945–4144* ⊕ *www. caymanvillas.com.*

Grand Cayman Villas. Virginia resident Jim Leavitt carries listings for dozens of fine properties islandwide. He and his staff visit the island regularly to ensure quality and remain up-to-date. ⊠ *846 Frank Sound Rd., George Town* ☎ *866/358–8455, 345/946–9524* ⊕ *www.grandcayman-villas.net.*

WIMCO. WIMCO, or the West Indies Management Company, is synonymous with quality throughout the world, especially the Caribbean. ☎ *888/997–3970* ⊕ *www.wimco.com.*

GEORGE TOWN AND ENVIRONS

If you are looking for a cheaper option and are willing to forego a beachfront location, there are a couple of guest-houses and simple hotels around George Town.

$$ ▣ **Sunset House.** *Hotel.* This amiable seaside dive-oriented resort is on the ironshore south of George Town, close enough for a short trip to stores and restaurants yet far enough to feel secluded. **Pros:** great shore diving and dive

CLOSE UP

Market Watch

Most condo and villa rentals start on Saturday. Since all the island's major supermarkets (and most other stores) close on Sunday, condo and villa renters may want to stop off for essentials right after they pick up their rental car. There are several American-style supermarkets near the airport, along West Bay Road parallel to Seven Mile Beach, and elsewhere in the island. *For specific listings, see Foodstuffs in Exploring Grand Cayman (with Shopping).* All stock fresh produce, poultry, and seafood; meats; baked goods; cold cuts and cheeses; hot and cold ready-made dishes at deli counters; and anything canned, frozen, and boxed. Just don't get sticker shock: prices average 25%–30% more than at home. If you expect to arrive on a Sunday or holiday when the supermarkets are closed, ask the condo resort or rental agent to arrange a starter kit.

Cayman Vacation Shoppers. Cayman Vacation Shoppers is a godsend for advance provisioning; it's also the only outfit on the island permitted to deliver wine and spirits on Sunday. ☎ *345/916–2978* 🌐 *www.caymanshoppers.com.*

shop; lively bar scene; fun international clientele; great package rates. **Cons:** often indifferent service; somewhat run-down; no real swimming beach; spotty Wi-Fi signal; five-night minimum stay required in high season. 💲 *Rooms from: $307* ✉ *390 S. Church St., George Town* ☎ *345/949–7111, 800/854–4767* 🌐 *www.sunsethouse.com* *58 rooms, 2 suites* 🍽 *Breakfast* ☞ *Five-night minimum stay in winter.*

SEVEN MILE BEACH

Most travelers to Grand Cayman choose to stay on one of the resorts or condo complexes along beautiful Seven Mile Beach. Although not all properties have a beachfront location, they are mostly in close proximity to the action and nearby restaurants, nightlife, and shops.

$$$$ **Beachcomber.** *Resort.* Beachcomber rose phoenix-like post-Ivan as a glam high-rise with 40 spacious two- to four-bedroom condos (roughly 24 in the rental pool). **Pros:** short walk to grocery stores, restaurants; on a great beach; high-tech amenities. **Cons:** no Wi-Fi on beach. 💲 *Rooms from: $1,025* ✉ *West Bay Rd., Seven Mile Beach* ☎ *345/943–6500* 🌐 *www.beachcomber.ky* *40 rooms.*

Seven Mile Beach

★ **Fodor's**Choice ⬚ **Caribbean Club.** *Rental.* This gleaming boutique
$$$$ facility has a striking lobby with aquariums, infinity pool,
and contemporary trattoria, Luca. **Pros:** luxurious, high-tech
facilities beyond the typical apartment complex; trendy Italian
restaurant; service on the beach. **Cons:** stratospheric prices;
poor bedroom reading lights; though families are welcome,
they may find it imposing; smaller top-floor balconies (albeit
amazing views). ⑤ *Rooms from: $1,256* ✉ *871 West Bay Rd.,
Seven Mile Beach* ☎ *345/623–4500, 800/941–1126* ⊕ *www.
caribclub.com* ⇌ *37 3-bedroom condos* ⑩ *No meals.*

$$$ ⬚ **Christopher Columbus.** *Rental.* This enduring favorite on
FAMILY the peaceful northern end of Seven Mile Beach is a find for
families. **Pros:** excellent snorkeling; fine beach; great value;
complimentary Wi-Fi. **Cons:** car needed; often overrun by
families during holidays and summer; top floors have diffi-
cult access for physically challenged. ⑤ *Rooms from: $415*
✉ *2013 West Bay Rd., Seven Mile Beach* ☎ *345/945–4354,
866/311–5231* ⊕ *www.christophercolumbuscondos.com*
⇌ *30 2- and 3-bedroom condos* ⑩ *No meals.*

$ ⬚ **Comfort Suites Grand Cayman.** *Hotel.* This no-frills, all-suites
hotel has an ideal location, next to the Marriott and near
numerous shops, restaurants, and bars. **Pros:** affordable; com-
plimentary buffet breakfast and Wi-Fi; fun, young-ish crowd.
Cons: rooms nearly a block from the beach; new condo blocks
sea views; no balconies; bar closes early. ⑤ *Rooms from: $252*
✉ *West Bay Rd., George Town* ☎ *345/945–7300, 844/229–
6267* ⊕ *www.caymancomfort.com* ⇌ *108 suites* ⑩ *Breakfast.*

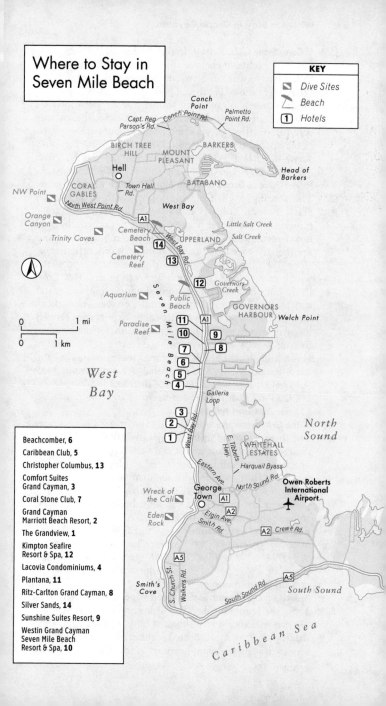

Where to Stay in Seven Mile Beach

KEY

◣ Dive Sites

⟋ Beach

1 Hotels

Conch Point

Palmetto Point Rd.

Capt. Reg Parson's Rd.

Conch Point Rd.

BIRCH TREE HILL

MOUNT PLEASANT

BARKERS

Head of Barkers

Hell ○

CORAL GABLES

Town Hall Rd.

BATABANO

NW Point ◣

North West Point Rd.

West Bay

Orange Canyon ◣

Little Salt Creek

Salt Creek

Trinity Caves ◣

Cemetery Beach

UPPERLAND

A1

14

Cemetery Reef ◣

13

Aquarium ◣

12

Public Beach

Governors Creek

GOVERNORS HARBOUR

Welch Point

Paradise Reef ◣

Seven Mile Beach

11

A1

10

9

7

8

6

5

4

Galleria Loop

North Sound

West Bay

0   1 mi

0   1 km

3

2

West Bay Rd.

1

WHITEHALL ESTATES

E. Tibbets Hwy.

Harquail Byass

Owen Roberts International Airport

Wreck of the Cali ◣

Eastern Ave.

George Town

A1

North Sound Rd.

Eden Rock ◣

A2

Elgin Ave.

Smith Rd.

A2

Crewe Rd.

Beachcomber, **6**

Caribbean Club, **5**

Christopher Columbus, **13**

Comfort Suites Grand Cayman, **3**

Coral Stone Club, **7**

Grand Cayman Marriott Beach Resort, **2**

The Grandview, **1**

Kimpton Seafire Resort & Spa, **12**

Lacovia Condominiums, **4**

Plantana, **11**

Ritz-Carlton Grand Cayman, **8**

Silver Sands, **14**

Sunshine Suites Resort, **9**

Westin Grand Cayman Seven Mile Beach Resort & Spa, **10**

Smith's Cove

S. Church St.

Walkers Rd.

A5

South Sound Rd.

A5

South Sound

Caribbean Sea

$$$$ ⬚ **Coral Stone Club.** *Rental.* In the shadow of the Ritz-Carlton, this exclusive enclave still shines by offering understated barefoot luxury, stellar service, and huge condos. **Pros:** large ratio of beach and pool space to guests; walking distance to restaurants and shops; free airport transfers; excellent off-season deals. **Cons:** expensive in high season; Ritz-Carlton guests sometimes wander over to poach beach space. ⑤ *Rooms from: $900* ✉ *985 West Bay Rd., Seven Mile Beach* ☎ *345/945–5820, 888/927–2322* ⊕ *www.coralstoneclub.com* ⮠ *30 3-bedroom condos* ⦿ *No meals.*

★ Fodor'sChoice ⬚ **Grand Cayman Marriott Beach Resort.** *Resort.*

$$$$ The soaring, stylish marble lobby (with exquisite art
FAMILY glass, majestic stingray bas relief sculpture, spectacular blown-up underwater photos, marine paraphernalia, and fun elements such as red British-style telephone boxes and apothecary cart dispensing "holistic handcrafted infusions") sets the tone for this bustling beachfront property, which received a $16-million renovation in 2015. **Pros:** lively bars and restaurants; good snorkeling and water sports; free bike and kayak rentals; convenient to both George Town and Seven Mile Beach; airport connectivity lets you print your boarding pass. **Cons:** often overrun by tour groups and conventioneers; narrowest section of Seven Mile Beach; beach sometimes washes out; pool and bar often noisy late; $50 resort fee. ⑤ *Rooms from: $489* ✉ *389 West Bay Rd., Seven Mile Beach* ☎ *345/949–0088, 800/223–6388* ⊕ *www.marriottgrandcayman.com* ⮠ *273 rooms, 22 suites* ⦿ *No meals.*

$$$ ⬚ **The Grandview.** *Rental.* Grand view, indeed: all 69 two-
FAMILY and three-bedroom units (sadly only 20 are generally in the rental pool) look smack onto the Caribbean and the beach past splendidly maintained gardens. **Pros:** restaurants and shops within walking distance; wine concierge dispenses advice; free Wi-Fi (when it's available); nice pool and hot tub. **Cons:** the long beach can be rocky; some units a tad worn though meticulously maintained; not all units have strong access to the free Wi-Fi signal. ⑤ *Rooms from: $475* ✉ *95 Snooze La., Seven Mile Beach* ☎ *345/945–4511, 866/977–6766* ⊕ *www.grandviewcondos.com* ⮠ *69 2- and 3-bedroom condos* ⦿ *No meals* ⌕ *5-night minimum high season.*

★ Fodor'sChoice ⬚ **Kimpton Seafire Resort + Spa.** *Resort.* Everything
$$$$ about the Seafire displays the Kimpton brand's trademark blend of elegance with a touch of funk, artfully adapted to the tropics. **Pros:** sophisticated without pretension; fabulous service; trademark complimentary extras like evening wine

tasting. **Cons:** high $60 resort fee; long walk from some rooms to public spaces; not ideal for guests with mobility issues. ⑤ *Rooms from: $599* ✉ *60 Tanager Way, Seven Mile Beach* ☎ *345/746–0000, 844/332–2112, 888/246–4412 toll-free reservations* ⤳ *266 rooms, 3 bungalows, 62 residences* ⍌ *No meals.*

$$$ ⌧ **Lacovia Condominiums.** *Rental.* The carefully manicured courtyard of this handsome arcaded Mediterranean Revival property could easily be mistaken for a peaceful park. **Pros:** central location; exquisite gardens; extensive beach. **Cons:** rear courtyard rooms can be noisy from traffic and partying from West Bay Road; pool fairly small (though most people prefer the beach). ⑤ *Rooms from: $415* ✉ *697 West Bay Rd., Seven Mile Beach* ☎ *345/949–7599* ⊕ *www.lacovia.com* ⤳ *35 1-, 2-, and 3-bedroom condos* ⍌ *No meals.*

$$$ ⌧ **Plantana.** *Rental.* Plantana is exceedingly lush, set on a stunning stretch of sand with smashing views of the leviathan ships lumbering into George Town and permeated with the sounds of surf and birdsong. **Pros:** Wi-Fi in rooms; great service; unique design. **Cons:** some rooms lack a nice view. ⑤ *Rooms from: $475* ✉ *1293 West Bay Rd., Seven Mile Beach* ☎ *345/945–4430* ⊕ *www.plantanacayman.com* ▭ *No credit cards* ⤳ *49 rooms.*

★ **Fodor'sChoice** ⌧ **Ritz-Carlton, Grand Cayman.** *Resort.* This 144-acre, exquisitely manicured resort, offers unparalleled luxury and service infused with a sense of place, with works by local artists and craftspeople. **Pros:** exemplary service; exceptional facilities with complimentary extras; fine beachfront. **Cons:** annoyingly high resort fee; sprawling with a confusing layout; long walk to beach (over an interior bridge) from most rooms. ⑤ *Rooms from: $1,299* ✉ *West Bay Rd., Seven Mile Beach* ☎ *345/943–9000* ⊕ *www.ritzcarlton.com* ⤳ *353 rooms, 12 suites, 24 condos* ⍌ *No meals.*
$$$$
FAMILY

$$$$ ⌧ **Silver Sands.** *Rental.* Silver Sands is an older compound that anchors the quieter northernmost end of Seven Mile Beach, with terrific snorkeling off the spectacular sweep of glittering sand. **Pros:** fabulous views; vaulted ceilings on second floor. **Cons:** lengthy minimum stay in winter; units are cramped. ⑤ *Rooms from: $595* ✉ *2131 West Bay Rd., Seven Mile Beach* ☎ *345/949–3343* ⊕ *www.silversandscayman.com* ▭ *No credit cards* ⤳ *42 rooms* ⌕ *Minimum stay is three nights summer, five in winter.*

$$ ⌧ **Sunshine Suites Resort.** *Hotel.* This friendly, all-suites hotel is an impeccably clean money saver. **Pros:** cheerful staff; rocking little restaurant; free access to business
FAMILY

Covered chaise longues at the Ritz-Carlton Grand Cayman

center and to nearby World Gym. **Cons:** poor views; not on the beach. ⑤ *Rooms from: $284* ✉ *1465 Esterley Tibbetts Hwy., off West Bay Rd., Seven Mile Beach* ☎ *345/949–3000, 877/786–1110* ⊕ *www.sunshinesuites. com* ⬦ *131 suites* ⦿ *Breakfast.*

★ Fodor'sChoice ☲ **The Westin Grand Cayman Seven Mile Beach Resort**
$$$$ **& Spa.** *Resort.* The handsomely designed, well-equipped
FAMILY Westin offers something for everyone, from conventioneers to honeymooners to families, not to mention what the hospitality industry calls "location location location." **Pros:** terrific children's programs; superb beach (the largest resort stretch at 800 feet); better-than-advertised ocean views; heavy online discounts. **Cons:** occasionally bustling and impersonal when large groups book; daily $50 resort fee. ⑤ *Rooms from: $699* ✉ *West Bay Rd., Seven Mile Beach* ☎ *345/945–3800, 800/937–8461* ⊕ *www.westingrandcayman.com* ⬦ *347 rooms,* ⦿ *No meals.*

WEST BAY

For those want to be out of the thick of things, yet still fairly close to Seven Mile Beach, there are a handful of resorts and condo rentals available in West Bay. Some of these even have waterfront locations, though they are fronted by ironshore rather than a sandy white beach.

$$ ☲ **Cobalt Coast Resort and Suites.** *Resort.* This small ecofriendly hotel is perfect for divers who want a moderately priced

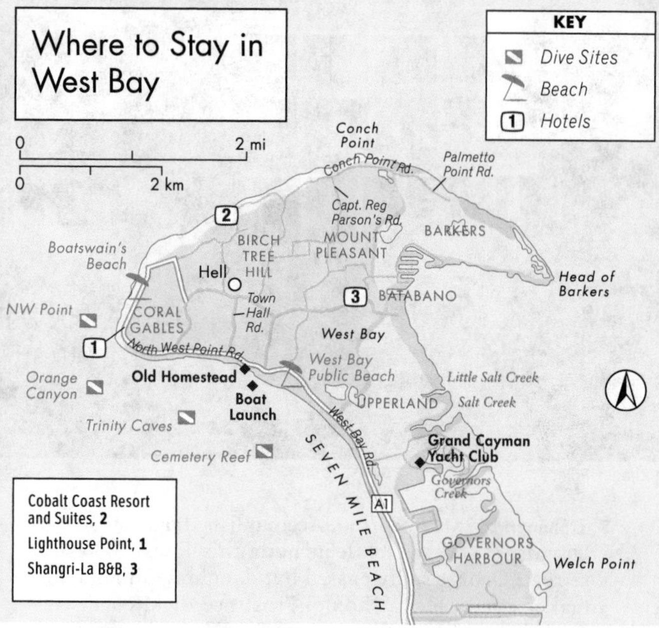

Where to Stay in West Bay
KEY
Dive Sites
Beach
1 Hotels
0
2 mi
0
2 km
Conch Point
Conch Point Rd.
Palmetto Point Rd.
Capt. Reg Parson's Rd.
MOUNT PLEASANT
BARKERS
Head of Barkers
BIRCH TREE HILL
Boatswain's Beach
Hell
Town Hall Rd.
3 BATABANO
NW Point
CORAL GABLES
West Bay
1
North West Point Rd.
2
Old Homestead
West Bay Public Beach
Little Salt Creek
Orange Canyon
Boat Launch
UPPERLAND
Salt Creek
Trinity Caves
West Bay Rd.
Grand Cayman Yacht Club
Cemetery Reef
SEVEN MILE BEACH
Governors Creek
A1
GOVERNORS HARBOUR
Welch Point
Cobalt Coast Resort and Suites, 2
Lighthouse Point, 1
Shangri-La B&B, 3

spacious room or suite right on the ironshore far from the madding crowds. **Pros:** superb dive outfit and packages; friendly service and clientele; free Wi-Fi; environmentally aware. **Cons:** poky golden-sand beach; unattractive concrete pool area; remote location, so a car (included in some packages) is necessary. *Rooms from: $290 ✉ 18-A Sea Fan Dr., West Bay ☎ 345/946–5656, 877/673–8820 🌐 www.cobaltcoast.com ⇆ 23 rooms, 🍽 Some meals.*

★ Fodor's Choice **Lighthouse Point.** *Resort.* Scuba operator Dive-
$$$ Tech's stunning ecodevelopment (motto "living lightly on the planet") features sustainable wood interiors and recycled concrete, a gray-water system, energy-saving appliances and lights, and Cayman's first wind turbine generator. **Pros:** eco-friendly; fantastic shore diving (and state-of-the-art dive shop); creative and often recycled upscale look; superb eatery. **Cons:** no real beach; car necessary; a bit difficult for physically challenged to navigate. *Rooms from: $450 ✉ 571 Northwest Point Rd., West Bay ☎ 345/949–1700 🌐 www.lighthouse-point-cayman.com, www.lighthousepointdiveresort.com ⇆ 9 2-bedroom apartments 🍽 No meals.*

Lighthouse Point

$ ☒ **Shangri-La B&B.** *B&B/Inn.* Accomplished pianist George Davidson and wife Eileen built this lavish lakeside retreat; George sadly passed but daughter Gillian truly makes guests feel at home. **Pros:** use of kitchen; elegant decor; DVD players and Wi-Fi included; rental bikes free. **Cons:** rental car necessary; not on the beach. ⑤ *Rooms from: $159* ✉ *1 Sticky Toffee La., West Bay* ☎ *345/526–1170* ⊕ *www.shangrilabandb.com* ⇘ *7 rooms, 1 apartment* ❢⧄ *Breakfast.*

EAST END

A stay in East End allows you to get away from the crowds and often stay on a lovely, sandy beach. The downside is a long drive into George Town or Seven Mile Beach of at least a half hour or 40 minutes.

$$ ☒ **Compass Point Dive Resort.** *Resort.* This tranquil, congenial getaway run by the admirable Ocean Frontiers scuba operation would steer even nondivers in the right direction. **Pros:** top-notch dive operation; free bike/kayak use; good value, especially packages; affable international staff and clientele; environmentally friendly, Green Globe–certified. **Cons:** isolated location requires a car; conservation is admirable but air-conditioning can't go too low; poky beaches with poor swim access. ⑤ *Rooms from: $295* ✉ *Austin Conolly Dr., East End* ☎ *345/947–7500, 800/348–6096, 345/947–0000*

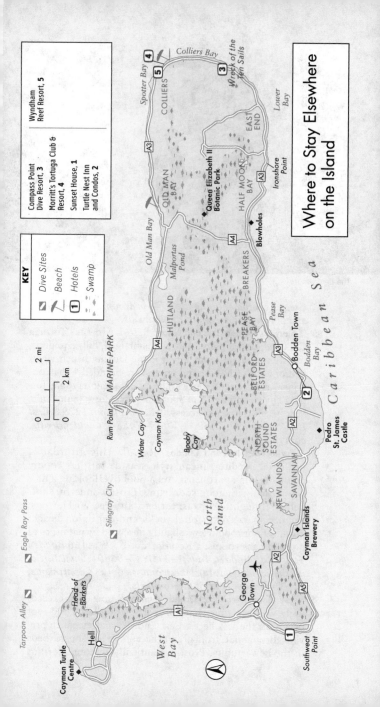

Where to Stay Elsewhere
on the Island

KEY

Dive Sites
Beach
1 Hotels
Swamp

Compass Point
Dive Resort, 3
Morritt's Tortuga Club &
Resort, 4
Sunset House, 1
Turtle Nest Inn
and Condos, 2

Wyndham
Reef Resort, 5

The Reef Resort

⊕ *www.compasspoint.ky* ⇌ *17 1-bedroom, 9 2-bedroom, and 3 3-bedroom condos* ⦿ *No meals.*

$$ ⬚ **Morritt's Tortuga Club and Resort.** *Resort.* Morritt's Tortuga Club and Resort offers 146 well-maintained, fully equipped, mostly timeshare units, albeit many lacking beach views and/or access (the best and priciest are branded "The Londoner" and "Grand Resort"). **Pros:** excellent day spa; Tortuga Divers and Red Sail Sports on site. **Cons:** many units lack beach views and access. ⑤ *Rooms from: $279* ⊠ *East End* ☎ *345/947–7449, 877/667–7488* ⊕ *www.morritts. com* ⇌ *146 rooms.*

$ ⬚ **Turtle Nest Inn and Condos.** *Rental.* This affordable, intimate, Mediterranean-style seaside inn has roomy one-bedroom apartments and a pool overlooking a narrow beach with good snorkeling. **Pros:** wonderful snorkeling; thoughtful extras; caring staff; free Wi-Fi. **Cons:** car necessary; occasional rocks and debris on beach; ground-floor room views slightly obscured by palms; road noise in back rooms. ⑤ *Rooms from: $199* ⊠ *166 Bodden Town Rd., Bodden Town* ☎ *345/947–8665* ⊕ *www.turtle-nestinn.com, www.turtlenestcondos.com* ⇌ *8 apartments, 10 2-bedroom condos* ⦿ *No meals.*

$$ ⬚ **Wyndham Reef Resort Grand Cayman.** *Resort.* This exceed-
FAMILY ingly well-run time-share property straddles a 600-foot beach on the less hectic East End. Casual elegance prevails throughout, from granite accents to four-poster beds in the newer units. **Pros:** romantically remote; glorious

beach; enthusiastic staff (including a crackerjack wedding coordinator); great packages and online discounts. **Cons:** remote; few dining options nearby; sprawling. ⑤ *Rooms from: $319* ✉ *2221 Queen's Hwy., Colliers* ☎ *345/947–3100, 888/232–0541* ⊕ *www.wyndhamcayman.com* ⇨ *152 suites* ⑩ *Some meals.*

GRAND CAYMAN
NIGHTLIFE AND
PERFORMING ARTS

Updated
by Jordan
Simon

DESPITE GRAND CAYMAN'S CONSERVATISM AND small size, the nightlife scene looms surprisingly large, especially on weekends. Choices include boisterous beach-and-brew hangouts, swanky wine bars, pool halls, sports bars, jammed and jamming dance clubs, live entertainment, and cultural events. A smoking ban was instituted in 2010 for nightspots and restaurants (one preexisting cigar bar and a hookah lounge received special dispensation).

Most major resorts, clubs, and bars offer some kind of performance, including lavish rum-and-reggae limbo/fire-eating/stilt-walking extravaganzas. Local bands with a fan(atic) following include soft-rock duo Hi-Tide; the Pandemonium Steelband; reggae-influenced trio Swanky; hard rockers Ratskyn (who've opened for REO Speedwagon, Mötley Crüe, and Bon Jovi); blues/funk purveyors Madamspeaker; and neo-punk rockers the Blow Holes. Other names to look for are Ka, l'Wild Knights, Island Vibes, C.I., Lammie, Heat, Gone Country, and Coco Red.

Consult the "Get Out" section in the Friday edition of the *Caymanian Compass* for listings of live music, movies, theater, and other entertainment. Local magazines such as *Key to Cayman, What's Hot,* and *Destination Cayman* can be picked up free of charge around the island, sometimes providing coupons for discounts and/or freebies. Bars remain open until 1 am, and clubs are generally open from 10 pm until 3 am, but they can't serve liquor after midnight on Saturday and they do not permit dancing on Sunday. Although shorts and sarongs are usually acceptable attire at beachside bars, smart casual defines the dress code for clubbing.

TIPSY TIPS. Don't drink and drive. Local police set sobriety checkpoints in heavily trafficked areas. The law is strict, the punishment (fine and/or prison) harsh. Watering holes will happily pour you into a taxi, or you can stick to the walkable cluster of bars in George Town and along Seven Mile Beach.

BEST BETS

■ **A Smokin' Time.** Even if you're not into stogies, Grand Cayman's cigar and wine bars are civilized hangouts where you might see stars or overhear insider trading tips.

■ **Local Rhythms.** Cayman's musicians have fanatic followings; it's worth a trip to The Wyndham Reef for the hilarious Barefoot Man. Lammie, Coco Red, Karen Edie, Gary Ebanks & Intransit, and Hi-Tide are other memorable musicians.

■ **Fish Feedings.** It's touristy, but watching tarpons pirou-

etting for bait at sunset reels even locals into waterfront watering holes.

■ **Culture Vultures.** If you want a real feel for Cayman life, take in an original play, particularly such annual special performances and festivals as Rundown and Gimistory.

■ **Full-Moon Parties.** Various beach bars host celebrations with almost pagan abandon, and these parties are overflowing with cocktails and camaraderie.

NIGHTLIFE

GEORGE TOWN

BARS AND MUSIC CLUBS

Cayman Cabana. The popular restaurant and bar (formerly Hammerheads), adorned with wild murals, fab old-timer photos, and surfboards doubling as signs, offers a classic Cayman sight: fishers anchor their boats right offshore and display their catch right outside (condo and villa renters, head here if you're in the market for fresh fish). The capable kitchen specializes in classic Caymanian cuisine; farm-to-table Thursdays are justifiably popular. This is also a prime pyrotechnic sunset- and cruise ship-watching spot, where locals laze in locally carved chairs, sipping house microbrews on the vast thatch-shaded, tiered deck. Stop by the Swanky Shack by the entrance for souvenir T-shirts and island gossip. ⊠ *N. Church St., George Town* ☎ *345/949–3080* ⊕ *www.caymancabanarestaurant.com.*

Hard Rock Café. Grand Cayman's Hard Rock replicates its 137-odd brethren around the world, only with more specialty drinks (try the Orangelicious margarita with Monin pomegranate and blood-orange juices) to complement its extensive burger selection. A 1960 pink Cadillac, a Madonna bullet bra, and rotating memorabilia (gold records, costumes, guitars, and autographed photos from Elton John, Korn, John Lennon, U2, and *NSYNC) are the decor. ⊠ *43 S. Church St., George Town* ☎ *345/947–2020* ⊕ *www.hardrock.com.*

Margaritaville. Grand Cayman's Margaritaville is a vast upstairs space that usually bustles with life (especially down its Green Monster waterslide or by its rooftop pool); the Friday evening happy hour is especially popular, with an overgrown frat-party atmosphere, and though drinks may be a bit pricier than at other waterfront locations, the jollity, 25 TVs, surprisingly tasty tacos, and free Wi-Fi definitely compensate. It closes early except on Friday nights. ⊠ *Anchorage Center, 32 Harbour Dr., 2nd fl., George Town* ☎ *345/949–6274* ⊕ *www.margaritavillecaribbean.com* ⊘ *Closed Sun.*

My Bar. Perched on the water's edge, this bar has great sunset views. The leviathan open-sided cabana is drenched in Rasta colors and crowned by an intricate South Seas–style thatched roof with about 36,000 palm fronds. Christmas lights and the occasional customer dangle from the rafters. They offer great grub, and the crowd is a mischievous mix of locals, expats, and tourists. ⊠ *Sunset House, S. Church St., George Town* ☎ *345/949–7111* ⊕ *www.sunsethouse.com.*

The Office Lounge. This is indeed a preferred hangout for the diverse after-work crowd, which packs both the cozy club space (adorned with customers' ties) and breezy patio, absorbing the high-octane cocktails and nightly musical mix (from country to salsa, karaoke to live bands). Happy hours are joyous indeed with CI$5 martini specials. It's invariably lively—a favorite spot for birthday, office, and bachelor and bachelorette parties and a prime place to eavesdrop on local gossip. ⊠ *99 Shedden Rd., George Town* ☎ *345/945–5212* ⊕ *www.tropicports.com/theoffice/.*

Rackam's Waterfront Pub and Restaurant. Both fishermen and financiers savor sensational sunsets and joyous happy hours, then watch tarpon feeding at this open-air, marine-theme bar on a jetty. Boaters and snorkelers, before and after checking out the wreck of *The Cali,* cruise up the ladder for drinks, while anglers leave their catch on ice. There's complimentary snacks on Friday and pub fare at fair prices until midnight. ⊠ *93 N. Church St., George Town* ☎ *345/945–3860* ⊕ *www.rackams.com.*

CLOSE UP

Caymans Captivating Carnival

Held annually during the first week of May (or the week after Easter), the four-day **Batabano Cayman Carnival** (⊕ *www. caymancarnival.com*) is the island's boisterous answer to Mardi Gras, not to mention Carnival in Rio and Trinidad. Though not as hedonistic, the pyrotechnic pageantry, electricity, and enthralled throngs are unrivaled (except for during Pirates Week). Events include a carnival ball, soca and calypso song competitions, massive Mas (masquerade) parade with ornate floats, street dance, and a beach fete. The festivities are enhanced by tasty concession stands offering Caymanian and other Caribbean cuisine and delicacies.

The word *batabano* refers to the tracks that turtles leave as they heave onto beaches to nest. Locating those tracks was reason to celebrate in the olden times, when turtling was a major part of the economy, so it seemed an appropriate tribute to the islands' heritage, alongside the traditional Caribbean celebration of the region's African roots. Indeed, many of the increasingly elaborate costumes are inspired by Cayman's majestic marine life and maritime history from parrots to pirates, though some offer provocative social commentary. Thousands of revelers line the streets each year cheering their favorite masqueraders and boogieing to the Mas steel pan and soca bands. The organizers also hold a stand-alone street parade for Cayman's youth called Junior Carnival Batabano the weekend before the adult parade. Equally exciting, it stresses the importance of teaching students the art of costume making and Mas, ensuring Carnival will be a lasting Caymanian custom.

The Wharf. Dance near the water to mellow music on Saturday evenings; when there's a wedding reception in the pavilion, the crashing surf and twinkling candles bathe the proceedings in an almost Gatsby-esque glow. For something less sedate, try salsa lessons and dancing on Tuesday after dinner; most Fridays morph into a wild 1970s disco night (after the free hors d'oeuvres served during happy hour). The legendary Barefoot Man (think a Jimmy Buffett–style expat) performs Saturdays. The stunning seaside setting on tiered decks compensates for often undistinguished food and service. The Ports of Call bar is a splendid place for sunset, and tarpon feeding off the deck happens every Monday at 7:30 and 9. ✉ *43 West Bay Rd., George Town* ☎ *345/949–2231* ⊕ *www.wharf.ky.*

SEVEN MILE BEACH

BARS AND MUSIC CLUBS

The Attic. This chic sports bar has three billiard tables, classic arcade games (Space Invaders, Donkey Kong), air hockey, and large-screen TVs (nab a private booth with its own flat-panel job). Events are daily happy hours, trivia nights, and the Caribbean's reputedly largest Bloody Mary bar on Sunday. Along with downstairs sister "O" Bar, it's ground zero for the Wednesday Night Drinking Club. For a $25 initiation (with T-shirt and personalized leather wristband, toga optional) and $10 weekly activity fee, you're shuttled by bus to three different bars, with free shots and drink specials. ⊠ *Queen's Court, 2nd fl., West Bay Rd., Seven Mile Beach* ☎ *345/949–7665.*

★ Fodor'sChoice **The Bar at Ave.** It's easy to overlook this bar at the entrance to the Seafire's main restaurant unless you're waiting for your table, but that would be a mistake. It's not the decor, which is surprisingly sterile despite the handsome driftwood sculpture hanging from the cathedral ceiling. Rather it's the remarkable mixologists who hold court, inventing cocktails on the spot based on your personality and preferences (if gregarious Spanish head bartender Juan-Manuel is there, you may end up camping out). You can also order dinner from the extensive regular Ave menu, including such standouts as crispy octopus with warm potato and white bean salad or cavatelli with rabbit ragu. ⊠ *Kimpton Seafire, 60 Tanager Way, Seven Mile Beach* ☎ *345/746–0000* ⊕ *www.seafireresortandspa.com.*

Calico Jack's. This friendly outdoor beach bar, seemingly glued together by license plates, pennants, and business cards, at the public beach's north end has a DJ on Saturday, open mike on Tuesday, live bands most Fridays, and riotous parties during the full moon. ⊠ *West Bay Rd., Seven Mile Beach* ☎ *345/945–7850.*

Deckers. Always bustling and bubbly, Deckers takes its name from the red English double-decker bus that forms the focal point of the main outdoor bar. You can luxuriate indoors on cushy sofas over a chess game and signature blood-orange mojito; hack your way through the 18-hole safari miniature-golf course; find a secluded nook in the garden terrace framed by towering palms, ornate street lamps, and colonial columns; or dance Thursday through Saturday night to pop, reggae, blues, and country courtesy of the Hi-Tide duo. Worthy Carib-Mediterranean fusion

Calico Jack's Bar and Grill

cuisine is a bonus (try the Caribbean lobster mac-and-cheese or the coconut shrimp with citrus marmalade and green papaya salad). Tuesday and Friday reel locals in for All-You-Can-Eat Lobster. ⊠ *West Bay Rd., Seven Mile Beach* ☎ *345/945–6600* ⊕ *www.deckers.ky.*

Duke's Seafood & Rib Shack. Half a block from the sand, Duke's embodies beach shack chic, with surfing photos, a reclaimed driftwood patio bar, and a statue of the big kahuna with shades and a board atop a manta ray. Locals and visitors belly up to the raw and real bars, especially at nightly happy hours, for "Cayman's endless summer." ⊠ *West Bay Rd., Seven Mile Beach* ⊹ *Across from public beach* ☎ *345/640–0000* ⊕ *www.dukescayman.com.*

Fidel Murphy's Irish Pub. Thanks to the unusual logo (a stogie-smoking Castro surrounded by shamrocks) and congenial Irish wit and whimsy, you half expect to find Raúl and Gerry Adams harping on U.S. and U.K. policy over a Harp. The Edwardian decor of etched glass, hardwood, and brass is prefabricated (constructed in Ireland, disassembled, and shipped), but everything else is genuine: the warm welcome, the ales and cider on tap, and the proper Irish stew (the kitchen also turns out conch fritters and lamb vindaloo). Sunday means all-you-can-eat extravaganzas (fish-and-chips, carvery) at rock-bottom prices. Trivia nights, happy hours, and live music lure regulars during the week. Weekends welcome live, televised Gaelic

A wall mural at the Havana Club Restaurant and Cigar Lounge

soccer, rugby, and hurling, followed by karaoke and *craic* (if you go, you'll learn the definition). ⊠ *Queen's Court, West Bay Rd., Seven Mile Beach* ☎ *345/949–5189* ⊕ *www. fidelmurphys.com.*

Legendz. This sports bar with a clubby, retro feel—Marilyn Monroe and Frank Sinatra photos channel glamour days, while scarlet booths and bubble chandeliers add oomph. Good luck wrestling a spot at the bar for pay-per-view and major sporting events, but 10 TVs, including two 6-by-8-foot screens, broadcast to every corner. Also an entertainment venue, Legendz books local bands, stand-up comics, and island DJs, and serves grilled fare at reasonable prices. ⊠ *Falls Centre, West Bay Rd., Seven Mile Beach* ☎ *345/943–3287* ⊕ *www.legendz.ky.*

Lone Star Bar and Grill. Calling itself Cayman's top dive, this bar is defined by its vast sports memorabilia collection, nearly 30 big-screen TVs tuned to different events, and excellent margaritas. Trivia and Rock 'n' Roll Bingo nights lasso locals. ⊠ *686 West Bay Rd., Seven Mile Beach* ☎ *345/945–5175* ⊕ *www.lonestarcayman.com.*

Stingers Resort and Pool Bar. Tasty, affordable food is served in an appealing setting (check out the stupendous "stinger" mosaic), with cover-free live music and dancing Thursday and Friday. On Wednesday is an all-you-can-eat Caribbean luau. The band Heat, local legends, sizzles with energetic,

Calling All Corsairs

For 11 days in November, Grand Cayman is transformed into a nonstop, fun-filled festivity. The annual **Pirates Week Festival** (⊕ www.piratesweek-festival.com) is the country's largest celebration, encompassing more than 30 different events including a kids' fun day, float parade, autocross, landing pageant, and underwater treasure hunt. You'll also encounter street dances, five heritage days (where various districts showcase their unique craft and culinary traditions), fireworks, song contests, costume competitions, cardboard-boat regattas, golf tournaments, swim meets, races, and teen music nights.

Everyone gets involved in the high-spirited high jinks (for example, dive boats stage mock battles and play practical jokes like filling the decks of "rivals" with cornflakes or jam, while swashbucklers "capture" hotel employees and guests). The opening night is an explosion of sights and sounds, from fireworks to rollicking bands before crowds of thousands in the George Town streets. Festivities last until the wee hours of the morning. Later in the week, another highlight is the mock pirate invasion of Hog Sty Bay and the spirited defense of the capital, culminating in the buccaneers' trial and extravagantly costumed street parades with ornate floats.

Most of the major events are free. The music sizzles, and the evening functions feature heaping helpings of yummy, affordable local fare (turtle stew, conch, jerk chicken). Given the enormous popularity of the festival, travelers should make reservations for hotel rooms and rental cars well in advance. Even taxis are in short supply for those wanting to attend the farther-flung heritage days. Hotels, shops, and the festival's administrative office do a brisk biz in corsair couture (though you can bring your own stuffed parrot and patch; just leave the sword at home).

emotional calypso, reggae, soca, salsa, and oldies; limbo dancers and fire-eaters keep the temperature rising. If you recoil from audience participation, stay far away. ⊠ *Comfort Suites Grand Cayman, West Bay Rd., Seven Mile Beach* ☎ *345/945–3000, 345/916–4402.*

CIGAR AND WINE LOUNGES

Havana Club Restaurant and Cigar Lounge. This venture from Cubano-phile Raglan Roper, who sailed his boat from Florida to Grand Cayman decades ago, is ironically smoke-free, though you can purchase Cuban cigars and cigarettes here (there's a small adjacent hut for fuming). The back lounge is intimate, with back-to-the-future touches like curved bars and chartreuse walls amid the handsome mahogany furnishings and vibrant Cuban artworks. Live musicians often animate weekend evenings; DJs spin three nights a week. A state-of-the-art ventilation system ensures the air remains clean. Best of all is meeting and admiring the dexterity of octogenarian Jesus Lara Perez, the in-house *torcedor,* or cigar roller, who started working in Cuban factories when he was 14 and has since traveled from the Bahamas to Belgium demonstrating his craft. ⊠ *Regency Court, 672 West Bay Rd., Seven Mile Beach* ☎ *345/945–5391, 345/946–5396* ⊕ *www.clubhavanacayman.com.*

Silver Palm Lounge. The Silver Palm drips with cash and cachet, with chic clientele. There's an old fashioned, leather-clad bar and another section that replicates a classic English country library (perfect for civilized, proper afternoon tea or a pre- or postdinner champagne or single malt). Also on tap: fab cocktails, including specialty martinis (the Silver Palm cosmopolitan is a winner—Ketel One citron, triple sec, a squeeze of fresh lime juice, and a splash of cranberry topped off with Moët champagne); pages of wines by the glass; and an impressive list of cigars, cognacs, and aged rums. ⊠ *Ritz-Carlton Grand Cayman, West Bay Rd., Seven Mile Beach* ☎ *345/943–9000* ⊕ *www.ritzcarlton.com/ GrandCayman.*

★ Fodor's Choice **West Indies Wine Company.** At this ultracontemporary wine store, purchasing tasting cards allows you to sample any of the 80-odd wines and spirits, available by the sip or half or full glass via the argon-enhanced "intelligent dispensing system." Selections traverse a vast canny range of prices, regions, styles, and terroirs. The enterprising owners struck a deal with neighboring restaurants and gourmet shops to provide appetizers or cheese and charcuterie plates, best savored alfresco at the tables in front of the handsome space. Small wonder savvy locals congregate here after work or a movie at the nearby cineplex. ⊠ *Corner of Market St. and the Paseo, Camana Bay* ☎ *345/640–9492* ⊕ *www.wiwc.ky.*

DANCE CLUBS

"O" Bar. This trendy black-and-crimson, industrial-style dance club has mixed music (live on Saturdays), while juggling, flame-throwing bartenders—practically local celebs—flip cocktails every night. It's as close to a stand-and-pose

Barefoot Man

H. George Nowak, aka "Barefoot Man," is hardly your ordinary Calypsonian. The blond-haired German-born, self-described "Nashville musical reject" moved from Munich to North Carolina after his mother remarried an Air Force officer. But "the inveterate map lover" dreamed of island life.

He started his island-hopping career in the U.S. Virgin Islands, then Hawaii, then the Bahamas ("the smaller, less populated, the better"), finally settling in the Cayman Islands in 1971.

He was dubbed Barefoot Boy ("since the nicest pair of footwear I owned were my Voit diving flippers") in 1971. While he'll still throw in a country or blues tune, Barefoot came to love the calypso tradition, especially its double entendres and political commentary.

He'll regale you between sets or over beers with colorful anecdotes of island life.

Barefoot sums up his philosophy simply and eloquently in one of his most popular lyrics (add gentle reggae-ish lilt), "I wish I were a captain, Sailin' on the sea. I'd sail out to an island, Take you there with me. I'd throw away the compass, Oh what a dirty scheme. ... Someday I might wake up, realize where I am, dreamin' like some 10-year-old, out in Disneyland, There is no tomorrow when you're living in a dream."

milieu as you'll find on Cayman. An upper-level private loft is available by reservation. ⊠ *Queen's Court, West Bay Rd., Seven Mile Beach* ☎ *345/943–6227, 345/916–0676.*

WEST BAY

BARS AND MUSIC CLUBS

Macabuca Oceanside Tiki Bar. This classic beach bar has a huge deck over the water, thatched roof, amazing mosaic murals of waves, spectacular sunsets (and sunset-colored libations), and tiki torches illuminating the reef fish come evening. *Macabuca* means "What does it matter?" in the indigenous Antillean Taíno language, perfectly encapsulating the mellow vibe. Big-screen TVs, live bands and DJs on weekends, excellent pub grub, and daily specials (CI\$9 jerk dishes weekends; Monday all-night happy hour, DJ, and CI\$17 all-you-can-eat barbecue) lure everyone from well-heeled loafers to barefoot bodysurfers animatedly discussing current events and dive currents in a Babel of tongues. ⊠ *857 Northwest Point Rd., West Bay* ☎ *345/945–5217* ⊕ *www.crackedconch.com.ky.*

EAST END

BARS AND MUSIC CLUBS

The Beach Bar. This spot draws an eclectic group of dive masters, expats, honeymooners, and mingling singles. The knockout, colorful cocktails pack quite a punch, making the sunset last for hours. The bar dialogue is entertainment enough, but don't miss local legend, country-calypsonian Barefoot Man, when he plays "upstairs" at Tides—he's to Cayman what Jimmy Buffett is to Key West. ⊠ *Reef Resort, 2221 Queen's Hwy., Colliers* ☎ *345/947–3100* ⊕ *www. wyndhamcayman.com.*

South Coast Bar and Grill. This delightful seaside slice of old Cayman—grizzled regulars slamming down dominoes, fabulous sea views, old model cars, Friday-night dances to local legend Lammie, karaoke Saturdays with Elvis impersonator Errol Dunbar, and reasonably priced red conch chowder and jerk chicken sausage—is also a big politico hangout. Fascinating photos, some historical, show local scenes and personalities. The juke jives, from Creedence Clearwater Revival to Mighty Sparrow. ⊠ *Breakers, East End* ☎ *345/947–2517.*

PERFORMING ARTS

Grand Cayman mounts special events throughout the year. The Cayman National Orchestra performs in disparate venues from the Cracked Conch restaurant to First Baptist Church. There's a burgeoning theater scene. Many new works use religious themes as a launching pad for meditations on issues relevant to current events, such as the Cayman Drama Society (⊕ *caymandramasociety.wildapricot.org*), *The Judith Code*, updating the biblical heroine's story to a present-day London of TV talk-show hosts and terrorist coalitions; the company also produces stimulating children's fare (*Mort,* based on Terry Pratchett's *Discworld* novels about a young boy apprenticed to Death), as well as escapist crowd-pleasing revivals like *Hairspray* and *Grease.*

TELLING TALES. **The Cayman National Cultural Foundation started "Gimistory" as a means of preserving the rich but vanishing oral tradition once passed from generation to generation. Held annually the last week of November, it features storytellers, often in elaborate garb, from Cayman and the Caribbean "spinnin' yarn" about old-time legends (duppies, spirits who return**

Preserving Caymans Cultural Heritage

Several worthy organizations are dedicated to keeping Caymanian traditions alive, including the National Trust of the Cayman Islands, which restores historic buildings and offers craft demonstrations and talks. The Cayman National Cultural Foundation mounts storytelling, musical, dance, and theatrical presentations, as well as readings and art exhibits that respect the "old ways" while seeking new forms of expression. The National Gallery also seeks to ensure vibrant vital world-class artistic development.

Respected local artist Chris Christian (who curates the Ritz-Carlton Gallery exhibits), cofounded **Cayman Traditional Arts** (*CTA, 60 W. Church St., West Bay, 345/946–0117,* *artcayman.blogspot.com*), which offers interactive classes for children and adults interested in learning authentic Caymanian arts, crafts, and recipes: thatch weaving, kite making, gig making and spinning, rope making, and an old-style cookout on the wood-burning oven called a caboose are just some of the topics. The network of freelance artisans has practiced these traditional crafts and customs their entire lives, often handed down over several generations, and represent the best in their disciplines. You really get hands-on in CTA's "living museum" headquarters, a 1917 mauve-and-mint wattle-and-daub cottage with ironwood posts that also doubles as a studio for Chris and Carly Jackson.

as bogeymen, or Pierrot Grande, the clown dressed in a colorful patchwork quilt of rags) as well as their travels and experiences. Free admission includes Caymanian delicacies like conch fritters and swanky (lemonade), part of a culinary competition.

VENUES

Harquail Theatre. This state-of-the-art facility seats 330 for theatrical performances, concerts, dance recitals, fashion shows, beauty pageants, art exhibits, and poetry readings sponsored by the Cayman National Cultural Foundation. ✉ *17 Harquail Dr., George Town* ☎ *345/949–5477*.

Lions Centre. The center hosts events throughout the year: Battle of the Bands competitions, concerts by top names on the Caribbean and international music scene such as Maxi Priest, stage productions, pageants, and sporting events. ✉ *Crewe Rd., Red Bay Estate* ☎ *345/945–4667, 345/949–7211.*

Prospect Playhouse. A thrust proscenium stage allows the Cayman Drama Society and its partner arts organizations to mount comedies, musicals, and dramas (original and revival) year-round. ✉ *223B Shamrock Rd., Prospect* ☎ *345/947–1998, 345/949–5054* ⊕ *www.cds.ky.*

GRAND CAYMAN SPORTS AND OUTDOOR ACTIVITIES

Updated
by Jordan
Simon

WATER, WATER, AND STILL MORE water rippling from turquoise to tourmaline; underneath lies nature's even more kaleidoscopically colorful answer to Disney World for scuba divers and snorkelers. The Cayman Islands' early aggressive efforts on behalf of marine conservation paid off by protecting some of the most spectacular reefs in the Western Hemisphere. There are innumerable ways to experience their pyrotechnics without getting your feet or hair wet, from submarines to glass-bottom boats, and a bevy of water sports: windsurfing, wrangling big-game fish, parasailing, and paddling kayaks through mangrove swamps.

Although most activities on Grand Cayman are aquatic in nature, landlubbers can do more than just loll on the lovely beaches. There are nature hikes, bird-watching treks, and horseback rides through the island's wilder, more remote areas. The golf scene is well above par for so small an island, with courses designed by Jack "The Golden Bear" Nicklaus and, fittingly, "The White Shark" Greg Norman. Even the most seasoned sea salts might enjoy terra firma, at least for half a day.

BEACHES

Grand Cayman is blessed with many beaches, ranging from cramped, untrammeled coves to long stretches basking like a cat in the sun, lined with bustling bars and water-sports concessions. All beaches are public, though access can be restricted by resorts.

GEORGE TOWN AND ENVIRONS

Cemetery Beach. A narrow, sandy driveway takes you past the small cemetery to a perfect strand just past the northern end of Seven Mile Beach. The dock here is primarily used by dive boats during winter storms. You can walk in either direction. The sand is talcum-soft and clean, the water calm and clear (though local surfers take advantage of occasional small reef breaks), and the bottom somewhat rocky and dotted with sea urchins, so wear reef shoes if wading. You'll definitely find fewer crowds. **Amenities:** none. **Best for:** snorkeling; solitude; surfing. ⊠ *West Bay Rd., Seven Mile Beach.*

Smith's Cove. South of the Grand Old House, this tiny but popular protected swimming and snorkeling spot makes a wonderful beach wedding location. The bot-

BEST BETS

■ **A Ray-diant Experience.** Feeding and petting the silky denizens of Stingray City and Stingray Sandbar are highlights of any Cayman trip.

■ **Snorkeling or Diving from Shore.** Explore the pyrotechnic reef life glittering just offshore all three islands.

■ **Hiking the Mastic Trail.** The ecocentric should hike (and sometimes hack their way) through this mix of ecosystems, including ancient dry forest that embraces 716 plant species as well as (harmless) wildlife.

■ **Putting on the Nightlights.** Kayak when the moon is waning to a bioluminescent bay; millions of microorganisms glow like fireflies.

tom drops off quickly enough to allow you to swim and play close to shore. Although slightly rocky (its pitted limestone boulders resemble Moore sculptures), there's little debris and few coral heads, plenty of shade, picnic tables, restrooms, and parking. Surfers will find decent swells just to the south. Note the curious obelisk cenotaph "In memory of James Samuel Webster and his wife Arabella Antoinette (née Eden)," with assorted quotes from Confucius to John Donne. **Amenities:** parking (no fee); toilets. **Best for:** snorkeling; sunset; swimming. ⊠ *Off S. Church St., George Town.*

SEVEN MILE BEACH

★ FodorsChoice **Seven Mile Beach.** Grand Cayman's west coast is dominated by this famous beach—actually a 6½-mile (10-km) expanse of powdery white sand overseeing lapis water stippled with a rainbow of parasails and kayaks. Free of litter and pesky peddlers, it's an unspoiled (though often crowded) environment. Most of the island's resorts, restaurants, and shopping centers sit along this strip. The public beach toward the north end offers chairs for rent ($10 for the day, including a beverage), a playground, water toys aplenty, beach bars, restrooms, and showers. The best snorkeling is at either end, by the Marriott and Treasure Island or off Cemetery Beach, to the north. **Amenities:** food and drink; showers; toilets; water sports. **Best for:** partiers; snorkeling. ⊠ *West Bay Rd., Seven Mile Beach.*

WEST BAY

Barkers. Secluded, spectacular beaches are accessed via a dirt road just past Papagallo restaurant. There are no facilities (that's the point!), but some palms offer shade. Unfortunately, the shallow water and rocky bottom discourage swimming, and it can be cluttered at times with seaweed and debris. You may also encounter wild chickens (their forebears released by owners fleeing Hurricane Ivan in 2004). Kitesurfers occasionally come here for the gusts. **Amenities:** none. **Best for:** solitude; walking; windsurfing. ⊠ *Conch Point Rd., Barkers, West Bay.*

NORTH SIDE

Old Man Bay. The North Side features plenty of hidden coves and pristine stretches of perfect sand, where you'll be disturbed only by seabirds dive-bombing for lunch and the occasional lone fishers casting nets for sprats, then dumping them into buckets. Over the Edge restaurant is less than 1 mile (1½ km) west. Otherwise, it's fairly undeveloped for miles, save for the occasional private home. Snorkeling is spectacular when waters are calm. **Amenities:** food and drink. **Best for:** snorkeling; solitude; walking. ⊠ *Queen's Hwy., North Side* ✣ *Just off Frank Sound Rd.*

Rum Point. This North Sound beach has hammocks slung in towering casuarina trees, picnic tables, casual and "fancier" dining options, a well-stocked shop for seaworthy sundries, and Red Sail Sports, which offers various water sports and boats to explore Stingray City. The barrier reef ensures safe snorkeling and soft sand. The bottom remains shallow for a long way from shore, but it's littered with small coral heads, so be careful. The Wreck is an ultracasual hangout serving outstanding pub grub from fish-and-chips to wings, as well as lethal Mudslide cocktails. Just around the bend, another quintessential beach hangout, Kaibo, rocks during the day. **Amenities:** food and drink; parking (no fee); showers; toilets; water sports. **Best for:** partiers; snorkeling. ⊠ *Rum Point, North Side.*

EAST END

East End Beaches. Just drive along and look for any sandy beach, park your car, and enjoy a stroll. The vanilla-hue stretch at Colliers Bay, by the Reef and Morritt's resorts (which offer water sports), is a good, clean one with superior snorkeling. **Amenities:** food and drink; water sports. **Best for:** snorkeling; solitude; sunrise; walking. ⊠ *Queen's Hwy., East End.*

SPORTS AND ACTIVITIES

BIKING

Mountain bikers will be disappointed by pancake-flat Grand Cayman, but cyclists looking to feel the burn while traversing varied scenery will be pleasantly surprised. The island's extremes, West Bay and East End, are most conducive to letting it fly.

FAMILY **Cycle Cayman.** This company rents top-notch cruisers, hybrids, and road bikes for $40–$100 per day, with deep weekly discounts. Their affable, knowledgeable staff also organizes tremendous three-hour West Bay Loops tours ($70) that double as an intriguing introduction to the area's farming and fishing heritage. Don't be surprised if Richard McKee, the lead tour guide and an avid historian, suggests a Caribbean reading list. ⊠ *Cracked Conch restaurant, 857 North West Point Rd., West Bay* ☎ *345/939–0911* ⊕ *www. westbayloop.com.*

Eco Rides Cayman. Green excursions that don't cost too many greenbacks are the house specialty, winding through the serene East End. The five routes ($70–$100) run from a scenic coastal route hugging the littoral without stopping, to a "cave trek" and "inland escape" that showcases natural topography—caverns, blowholes, and local farms. Rentals available upon request. ⊠ *2708 Seaview Dr., East End* ☎ *345/922–0754* ⊕ *www.ecoridescayman.ky.*

6

BIRD-WATCHING

The Cayman Islands are an ornithologist's dream, providing perches for a wide range of resident and migratory birds— 219 species at last count, many of them endangered, such as the Cayman parrot. The National Trust organizes regular bird-watching field trips conducted by local ornithologists through the Governor Michael Gore Bird Sanctuary, Queen Elizabeth II Botanic Park, Mastic Reserve, Salina Reserve, Central Mangrove Wetland, Meagre Bay Pond Reserve in Pease Bay, Colliers Pond in East End, and Palmetto Pond at Barkers in West Bay. Prime time for bird-watching is either early in the morning or late in the afternoon; take strong binoculars and a field guide to identify the birds.

DIVING

One of the world's leading dive destinations, Grand Cayman has dramatic underwater topography that features plunging walls, soaring skyscraper pinnacles, grottoes, arches, swim-throughs adorned with vibrant sponges, coral-encrusted caverns, and canyons patrolled by lilliputian grunts to gargantuan groupers, darting jacks to jewfish, moray eels to eagle rays. Gorgonians and sea fans wave like come-hither courtesans. Pyrotechnic reefs provide homes for all manner of marine life, ecosystems encased within each other like an intricate series of Chinese boxes.

Reef Watch. This progressive program, a partnership between the Department of the Environment and Cayman Islands Tourism Association, debuted in 1997 during Earth Day activities. The DOE designed a field survey to involve diving and snorkeling tourists in counting and cataloging marine life. To date, more than 1,000 surveys have been completed, helping to estimate species' populations and travel patterns based on sightings and their distance from buoys and other markers, as well as gauging how often equipment touches the fragile reefs. Though not scientifically sound, it does enhance awareness through interaction.

DIVE SITES

There are more than 200 near-pristine dive sites, many less than a half mile from the island and easily accessible, including wreck, wall, and shore options. Add exceptional visibility from 80 to 150 feet (no rivers deposit silt) and calm, current-free water at a constant bathlike 80°F. Cayman is serious about conservation, with stringently enforced laws to protect the fragile, endangered marine environment (fines up to $500,000 and a year in prison for damaging living coral, which can take years to regrow), protected by the creation of Marine Park, Replenishment, and Environmental Park Zones. Local water-sports operators enthusiastically cooperate: most boats use biodegradable cleansers and environmentally friendly drinking cups. Moorings at all popular dive sites prevent coral and sponge damage due to continual anchoring; in addition, diving with gloves is prohibited to reduce the temptation to touch.

Pristine water, breathtaking coral formations, and plentiful marine life including hammerheads and hawksbill turtles mark the **North Wall**—a world-renowned dive area along the North Side of Grand Cayman.

Learn to Dive

Diving is an exciting experience that does not have to be strenuous or stressful. Almost anyone can enjoy scuba, and it's easy to test the waters via a three-hour resort course costing $110–$150, including one or two dives. After a quick rundown of dos and don'ts, you stand in the shallow end of a pool, learning how to use the mask and fins and breathe underwater with a regulator. The instructor then explains some basic safety skills, and before you know it you're in the drink. The instructor hovers as you float above the reef, watching fish react to you. Don't worry—there are no dangerous fish in Cayman, and they don't bite (as long as you're not "chumming," or handling fish food). You can see corals and sponges, and maybe even a turtle or ray.

The resort course only permits shallow, instructor-guided dives in Cayman's calm, clear waters. The next step is full Open Water certification (generally three to four days, including several dives, for around $500, less as part of a hotel package). This earns you a C-card, your passport to the underwater world anywhere you travel. From there, addicts will discover dozens of specialty courses. The leading teaching organizations, both with their adherents, are PADI (Professional Association of Dive Instructors) and NAUI (National Association of Underwater Instructors), affectionately nicknamed "Pay and Dive Immediately" and "Not Another Underwater Idiot" (those are the polite versions in scuba's colorful slang). Worry not: Cayman's instructors are among the world's best. And the water conditions might just spoil you.

Trinity Caves in West Bay is a deep dive with numerous canyons starting at about 60 feet and sloping to the wall at 130 feet. The South Side is the deepest, with the top of its wall starting 80 feet deep before plummeting, though its shallows offer a lovely labyrinth of caverns and tunnels in such sites as **Japanese Gardens** and **Della's Delight**.

The less-visited, virgin East End is less varied geographically beyond the magnificent **Ironshore Caves** and **Babylon Hanging Gardens** (trees of black coral plunging 100 feet), but it teems with "Swiss-cheese" swim-throughs and exotic life in such renowned gathering spots as **The Maze** (a hangout for reef, burse, and occasional hammerhead sharks), **Snapper Hole,** and **Grouper Grotto.**

The Cayman Islands government acquired the 251-foot, decommissioned USS *Kittiwake* (⊕ *www.kittiwakecayman. com*). Sunk in January 2011, it has already become an exciting new dive attraction, while providing necessary relief for some of the most frequently visited dive sites. The top of the bridge is just 15 feet down, making it accessible to snorkelers. There's a single-use entry fee of $10 ($5 for snorkelers).

The **Cayman Dive 365** (⊕ *www.dive365cayman.com*) initiative is part of a commitment to protect reefs from environmental overuse. New dive sites will be introduced while certain existing sites are "retired" to be rested and refreshed. Visitors are encouraged to sponsor and name a new dive site from the list of selected coordinates.

★ Fodor'sChoice **Stingray City.** Most dive operators offer scuba trips to Stingray City in the North Sound. Widely considered the best 12-foot dive in the world, it's a must-see for adventurous souls. Here dozens of stingrays congregate— tame enough to suction squid from your outstretched palm. You can stand in 3 feet of water at **Stingray City Sandbar** as the gentle stingrays glide around your legs looking for a handout. Don't worry—these stingrays are so acclimated to tourist encounters that they pose no danger; the experience is often a highlight of a Grand Cayman trip. ⊠ *Near West Bay, North Sound.*

SHORE DIVING

Shore diving around the island provides easy access to kaleidoscopic reefs, fanciful rock formations, and enthralling shipwrecks. The areas are well marked by buoys to facilitate navigation. If the water looks rough where you are, there's usually a side of the island that's wonderfully calm.

★ Fodor'sChoice **Devil's Grotto.** This site resembles an abstract painting of anemones, tangs, parrot fish, and bright purple Pederson cleaner shrimp (nicknamed the dentists of the reef, as they gorge on whatever they scrape off fish teeth and gills). Extensive coral heads and fingers teem with blue wrasse, horse-eyed jacks, butterfly fish, and Indigo hamlets. The cathedral-like caves are phenomenal, but tunnel entries aren't clearly marked, so you're best off with a dive master. ⊠ *George Town.*

★ Fodor'sChoice **Eden Rock.** If someone tells you that the silverside minnows are in at Eden Rock, drop everything and dive here. The schools swarm around you as you glide through

Dive Tips

Here are a few helpful hints to maximize your enjoyment:

■ If you're not strong, ask someone to carry your tank and don't go in rough water from shore.

■ Always orient yourself on the sandy bottom near the boat: check gauges and camera/video equipment, fine-tune your buoyancy, and ensure that your buddy is also secure.

■ Use a flashlight to explore crevices and illuminate the true dazzling colors of soft corals, sponges, and tunicates.

■ Check overhangs and outcroppings where grouper, tarpon, minnows, and other fish hang out in the shade.

■ Never touch black coral, usually found near 100-foot depths under outcroppings or inside tunnels. It's quite fragile, growing a mere inch every two to three years.

■ Fire coral is prevalent in the tropics and assumes many forms. Skin contact is painful (explaining the name). Vinegar or isopropyl alcohol helps alleviate pain; hydrocortisone cream or gel ameliorates the itch.

■ When shore diving off George Town, always use a surface float marker to indicate your position to the snorkeler/boater traffic.

■ If you become fatigued, float on your back; the seawater buoys you.

the grottoes, forming quivering curtains of liquid silver as shafts of sunlight pierce the sandy bottom. The grottoes themselves are safe—not complex caves—and the entries and exits are clearly visible at all times. Snorkelers can enjoy the outside of the grottoes as the reef rises and falls from 10 to 30 feet deep. Avoid carrying fish food or risk getting bitten by eager yellowtail snappers. ⊠ *S. Church St., George Town* ✛ *Across from Harbour Place Mall, by Paradise Restaurant.*

Turtle Reef. The reef begins 20 feet out and gradually descends to a 60-foot miniwall pulsing with sea life and corals of every variety. From there it's just another 15 feet to the dramatic main wall. Ladders provide easy entrance to a shallow cover perfect for predive checks, and because the area isn't buoyed for boats, it's quite pristine. ⊠ *West Bay.*

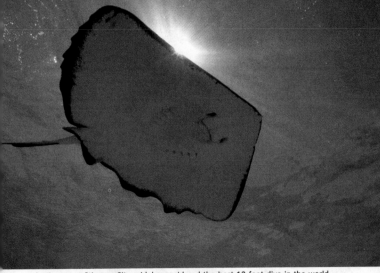

A stingray at Stingray City, widely considered the best 12-foot dive in the world

DIVE OPERATORS

As one of the Caribbean's top diving destinations, Grand Cayman is blessed with many top-notch dive operations offering diving, instruction, and equipment for sale and rent. A single-tank boat dive averages $80, a two-tank dive $105–$129 (with discounts for multiday packages). Snorkel-equipment rental is about $15 a day. Divers are required to be certified and possess a "C" card. If you're getting certified, to save time during your limited holiday you can start the book and pool work at home and finish the open-water portion in warm, clear Cayman waters. Certifying agencies offer this referral service all around the world.

When choosing a dive operator, ask if they require that you stay with the group, and whether they provide towels, camera rinse water, protection from inclement weather, tank-change service, beach or resort pickup, and/or snacks between dives. Ask what dive options they have during a winter storm (called a nor'wester here), as well as what kind of boat they use. Don't assume that a small, less crowded boat is better. Some large boats are more comfortable, even when full, than a tiny, uncovered boat without a marine toilet. Small boats, however, offer more personal service and less-crowded dives.

Strict marine protection laws prohibit you from taking any marine life from many areas around the island. Always check with the **Department of Environment** (*345/949–8469*) before diving, snorkeling, and fishing. To report violations, call **Marine Enforcement** (*345/948–6002*).

Ambassador Divers. This on-call (around the clock), guided scuba-diving operation offers trips for two to eight persons. Co-owner Jason Washington's favorite spots include sites on the West Side and South and North Wall. Ambassador offers three boats: a 28-foot custom Parker (maximum six divers), a 46-foot completely custom overhauled boat, and a 26-footer primarily for snorkeling. Divers can be picked up from their lodgings. A two-tank boat dive is $115. ⊠ *Comfort Suites, 22 Piper Way, West Bay Rd., Seven Mile Beach* ☎ *345/743–5513, 345/949–4530, 844/507–0441 toll-free* ⊕ *www.ambassadordivers.com.*

Cayman Aggressor IV. This 110-foot live-aboard dive boat offers one-week cruises for divers who want to get serious bottom time, as many as five dives daily. Nine staterooms with bathrooms en suite sleep 18. The fresh food is basic but bountiful (three meals, two in-between snacks), and the crew offers a great mix of diving, especially when weather allows the crossing to Little Cayman. Digital photography and video courses are also offered (there's an E-6 film-processing lab aboard) as well as nitrox certification. The price is $2,795 to $3,295 double occupancy for the week. ☎ *345/949–5551, 800/348–2628* ⊕ *www.aggressor.com.*

★ Fodor's Choice **DiveTech.** With comfortable boats and quick
FAMILY access to West Bay, DiveTech offers shore diving at its northwest-coast location, providing loads of interesting creatures, a miniwall, and the North Wall. Technical training (a specialty of owner Nancy Easterbrook) is unparalleled, and the company offers good, personable service as well as the latest gadgetry such as underwater DPV scooters and rebreathing equipment. They even mix their own gases. Options include extended cross-training Ranger packages, Dive and Art workshop weeks, photography-video seminars with Courtney Platt, deep diving, free diving, search and recovery, stingray interaction, reef awareness, and underwater naturalist. Snorkel and diving programs are available for children eight and up, SASY (supplied-air snorkeling, with the unit on a personal flotation device) for five and up. Multiday discounts are a bonus. ⊠ *Lighthouse Point , 571 Northwest Point Rd., West Bay ✢ Near Boatswain's Beach* ☎ *345/949–1700, 877/946–5658* ⊕ *www.divetech.com.*

6

Divers exploring one of Grand Cayman's famous reefs

Don Foster's Dive Cayman Islands. This operation offers a pool with shower, an underwater photo center, and snorkeling along the ironshore at Casuarina Point, easily accessed starting at 20 feet and extending to 55 feet. Night dives and Stingray City trips take divers and snorkelers in the same boat (good for families). Specialties include Nitrox, Wreck, and Peak Performance Buoyancy courses. Rates are competitive, and there's free shuttle pickup–drop-off along Seven Mile Beach. If you go out with Don, he might recount stories of his wild times as a drummer, but all crews are personable and efficient. The drawback is larger boats and groups. ⊠ *218 S. Church St., George Town* ☎ *345/949–5679, 345/945–5132* ⊕ *www.donfosters.com.*

★ **Fodor'sChoice** **Indigo Divers.** This full-service, mobile PADI teaching facility specializes in exclusive guided dives from its 28-foot Sea Ray Bow Rider or 32-foot Stamas, the *Cats Meow* and the *Cats Whiskers*. Comfort and safety are paramount. Luxury transfers are included, and the boat is stocked with goodies like fresh fruit and homemade cookies. Captain Chris Alpers has impeccable credentials: a licensed U.S. Coast Guard captain, PADI master scuba diver trainer, and Cayman Islands Marine Park officer. Katie Alpers specializes in wreck, DPV, dry suit, boat, and deep diving, but her primary role is videographer. She edits superlative DVDs of the adventures with music and titles. They guarantee a maximum of six divers. The individual attention is pricier; larger the group, the more you save. ⊠ *Seven Mile Beach* ☎ *345/946–7279, 345/525–3932* ⊕ *www.indigodivers.com.*

Neptune's Divers. Offering competitive package rates and free shuttle service along Seven Mile Beach, this is one of the best companies for physically challenged divers. Captain Keith Keller and his staff try to customize trips as best they can, taking no more than eight divers on their 30-foot custom Island Hopper and 36-foot Crusader. A wide range of PADI courses is available. Instructors are patient and knowledgeable about reef life, and Casey Keller can offer helpful tips on underwater photography. The operation is computer-friendly to permit longer bottom time. ⊠ *West Bay Rd., Seven Mile Beach* ☎ *345/945–3990* ⊕ *www.neptunesdivers.com.*

★ **Fodor'sChoice Ocean Frontiers.** This excellent ecocentric operation offers friendly small-group diving and a technical training facility, exploring the less trammeled, trafficked East End. The company provides valet service, personalized attention, a complimentary courtesy shuttle, and an emphasis on green initiatives and specialized diving, including unguided computer, technical, nitrox instructor, underwater naturalist, and cave diving for advanced participants. You can even participate in lionfish culls. There's a wonderful Skills Review and Tune-Up course so beginners or rusty divers won't feel over their heads. Special touches include hot chocolate and homemade muffins on night dives; the owner, Steve, will arrange for a minister to conduct weddings in full face masks. ⊠ *Compass Point, 346 Austin Connelly Dr., East End* ☎ *345/640–7500, 800/348–6096 toll-free, 345/947–0000, 954/727–5312 Vonage toll-free in U.S.* ⊕ *www.oceanfrontiers.com.*

FAMILY Red Sail Sports. Daily trips leave from most major hotels, and dives are often run as guided tours, good for beginners. If you're experienced and your air lasts long, ask the captain if you must come up with the group (when the first person runs low on air). Kids' options, ages 5 to 15, include SASY and Bubblemakers. The company also operates Stingray City tours, dinner and sunset sails, and water sports from Wave Runners to windsurfing. ☎ *345/949–8745, 345/623–5965, 877/506–6368* ⊕ *www.redsailcayman.com.*

Sunset Divers. At a hostelry that caters to the scuba set, this full-service PADI teaching facility has great shore diving and six dive boats that hit all sides of the island. Divers can be independent on boats as long as they abide by maximum time and depth standards. Instruction (in five languages, thanks to the international staff) and stay-dive packages are comparatively inexpensive. Though the company is not directly affiliated with acclaimed underwater shutterbug Cathy Church (whose shop is also at the hotel), she often works with the instructors on special courses. ✉ *Sunset House, 390 S. Church St., George Town* ☎ *345/949–7111, 800/854–4767* ⊕ *www.sunsethouse.com.*

FISHING

The Cayman Islands are widely hailed as a prime action-packed destination for all types of sportfishing, from casting in the flats for the wily, surprisingly strong "gray ghost" bonefish, to trolling for giant, equally combative blue marlin. Conditions are ideal for big game fish: the water temperature varies only 8 to 10 degrees annually, so the bait and their pelagic predators hang out all year. The big lure for anglers is the big game-fish run near the coast, as close as a quarter-mile offshore.

Experienced, knowledgeable local captains charter boats with top-of-the-line equipment, bait, ice, and often lunch included in the price (usually $550–$750 per half day, $900–$1,500 for a full day). Options include deep-sea, reef, bone, tarpon, light-tackle, and fly-fishing. June and July are particularly good all-around months for reeling in blue marlin, yellow- and blackfin tuna, dolphinfish (dorado), and bonefish. Bonefish have a second season in the winter months, along with wahoo and skipjack tuna. Marine Park laws prohibit fishing or taking any type of marine life in protected areas. Local captains promote conservation and sportsmanship through catch-and-release of both reef and pelagic fish not intended for eating and all billfish, unless they are local records or potential tournament winners.

Oh Boy Charters. Charters include a 60-foot yacht with complete amenities (for day and overnight trips, sunset and dinner cruises) and a 34-foot Crusader. Charles and Alvin Ebanks—sons of Caymanian marine royalty, the indomitable Captain Marvin Ebanks—jokingly claim they've been playing in and plying the waters for a century and tell tales (tall and otherwise) of their father reeling them in for fishing expeditions. No more than eight passengers on the deep-sea boats ensures the personal touch (snorkeling on the 60-footer accommodates more people). Guests always

Learning In-Depth

Technical diving refers to advanced dives conducted beyond the 130-foot depth limit, requiring a decompression stop, or into an overhead environment. DiveTech's Nancy Easterbrook compares it to "skiing a really steep mogul-ly double black diamond, or scaling a sheer cliff face. It takes practice and determination." The courses and equipment are also much more expensive.

Terms you'll soon hear are *Nitrox, Advanced Nitrox, Normoxic, Trimix,* and *Advanced Trimix.* These all enable divers to explore deeper depths safely at greater length. Nitrox, for example, is highly oxygen-ated nitrogen (32% as opposed to "normal" air, with 21%), which enables you to dive for a longer time before reaching decompression limits. And just like the oxygen-bar craze of the last decade, Nitrox invigorates you, reducing fatigue after dives.

Rebreather diving (Closed Circuit Rebreathers, or CCR) is another popular way to extend dive time, up to three hours 100 feet down. You breathe warmer, moister air (reducing the chance of chills at lower depths). As a bonus, denizens of the deep are less wary, as there are no bubbles.

6

receive a good selection of their catch; if you prefer others to do the cooking, go night fishing (including catch-and-release shark safaris), which includes dinner. ☏ *345/949–6341, 345/926–0898* ⊕ *www.ohboycharters.com.*

R&M Fly Shop and Charters. Captain Ronald Ebanks is arguably the island's most knowledgeable fly-fishing guide, with more than 10 years' experience in Cayman and Scotland. He also runs light-tackle trips on a 24-foot Robalo. Everyone from beginners—even children—to experienced casters enjoy and learn, whether wading or poling from a 17-foot Stratos Flats boat. Free transfers are included. Captain Ronald even ties his own flies (he'll show you how). ☏ *345/947–3146, 345/916–5753 cell* ⊕ *www.fly-fishgrandcayman.com.*

GOLF

North Sound Golf Club. Formerly the Links at Safehaven, this is Cayman's only 18-hole golf course and infamous among duffers for its strong wind gusts. Roy Case factored the wind into his design, which incorporates lots of looming water and sand bunkers. The handsome setting features many mature mahogany and silver thatch trees where iguana lurk. Wear shorts at least 14 inches long (15 inches for women) and collared shirts. Greens fees change seasonally, and there are twilight and walking discounts (though carts are recommended), a fine pro shop, and an open-air bar with large-screen TVs. ✉ *557 Safehaven Dr., Seven Mile Beach* ✛ *Off West Bay Rd.* ☎ *345/947–4653* ⊕ *www.northsound-club.com* 💲 *$175 for 18 holes, $110 for 9 holes, including cart; twilight rates* ⚡ *18 holes, 6605 yards, par 71.*

Ritz-Carlton Golf Club. Designed by Greg Norman in 2006 and built on undulating terrain near mangroves, this lovely course, formerly dubbed Blue Tip, is now open to non-Ritz-Carlton guests as well. Five of the holes are par-4s, and two are par-5s, including a 600-yarder, so there is plenty of muscle to the layout. Abundant water hazards, tricky winds, and sudden shifts in elevation challenge most duffers. No jeans are allowed, and you must wear collared golf shirts. Club rentals are available at the golf shop. ✉ *Ritz-Carlton Grand Cayman, West Bay Rd., Seven Mile Beach* ☎ *345/943–9000, 345/815–6500* ⊕ *www.ritzcarlton.com* 💲 *$195 for 18 holes ($199 nonguests), $125 for 9 holes; twilight discounts* ⚡ *9 holes, 3515 yards, par 36.*

GUIDED TOURS

Taxi drivers will give you a personalized tour of Grand Cayman for about $25 per hour for up to three people. Or, you can choose a fascinating helicopter ride, a horseback or mountain-bike journey, a 4x4 safari expedition, or a full-day bus excursion. Ask your hotel to help you make arrangements.

Costs and itineraries for island tours are about the same regardless of the tour operator. Half-day tours average $40–$50 a person and generally include a visit to Hell and the Turtle Farm aquatic park in West Bay, as well as shopping downtown. Full-day tours ($60–$90 per person) add lunch, a visit to Bodden Town (the first settlement), and the East End, where you stop at the Queen Elizabeth II Botanic Park, blowholes (if the waves are high) on the ironshore, and the site of the wreck of the *Ten Sails* (not the wreck itself—just the site). The pirate graves in Bodden Town were destroyed during Hurricane Ivan in 2008, and the blowholes were partially filled. Children under 12 often receive discounts.

Turtles and Cats

Blessed with arguably the world's largest turtle nesting grounds, Cayman developed into the center of the Caribbean turtle industry for nearly two centuries. English settlers on Jamaica became particularly proficient turtlers. Once they hunted the population into near-extinction by the early 1800s, Caymanians went to sea for months, trapping and supplying turtles from Cuba and Nicaragua well into the 20th century. Even today roughly 20 locals are licensed to catch four turtles annually, and the Cayman Turtle Centre (an environmentally sensitive "working" part of the marine theme park formerly known as Boatswain's Beach) supplies the local market with farm-raised meat.

Turtling led indirectly to one of the proud Caymanian con-

tributions to shipbuilding, the catboat. The design of this basic sailboat (not a catamaran) is usually credited to Cayman Brac's Daniel Jervis circa 1904, though Cape Cod and Chesapeake Bay boaters debate the origin. He decided to bring the stern to a sharp point, similar to New England/Canadian whalers and peapods, placing the mast in the bow. Supposedly, the shape permitted quicker course reversal and less drag, while the lack of keel depth facilitated beaching the boat. Ballast provided stability, and only a yoke was used to steer the rudder.

The Cayman Catboat Club holds several annual regattas as well as free rides during special events, including Pirates Week.

6

A.A. Transportation Services. For taxis and tour buses, ask for Burton Ebanks. ☎ *345/926–8294, 345/949–7222* ⊕ *www. aatransportation.weebly.com.*

Cayman Safari. This hits the usual sights but emphasizes interaction with locals, so you learn about craft traditions, folklore, and herbal medicines; careening along in Land Rovers is incidental fun. Rates range from $79 to $99 ($69 to $79 for children under 12). ☎ *345/925–3002* ⊕ *www. caymansafari.com.*

Majestic Tours. The company caters mostly to cruise-ship and incentive groups but offers similar options to individuals and can customize tours, starting at $45 per person; it's particularly good for West Bay, including the Cayman Turtle Centre and Hell. ⊠ *Industrial Park, 322 N. Sound Rd.* ☎ *345/949–7773* ⊕ *www.majestictours.ky.*

McCurley Tours. This outfit is owned by B.A. McCurley, a free-spirited, freewheeling midwesterner who's lived in Cayman since the mid-1980s and knows everything and everyone on the East End. Not only is she encyclopedic and flexible, but she also offers car rentals and transfers for travelers staying on the North Side or East End; don't be surprised if she tells you what to order at lunch, especially if it's off the menu. ☎ *345/947-9626, 345/916-0925.*

Tropicana Tours. With several excellent itineraries on large buses, tours include Stingray City stops as well as reef runner adventures across the North Sound through the mangrove swamps. ☎ *345/949-0944 ⊕ www.tropicana-tours.com.*

HIKING

Mastic Trail. This significant trail, used in the 1800s as the only direct path to the North Side, is a rugged 2-mile (3-km) slash through 776 dense acres of woodlands, black mangrove swamps, savanna, agricultural remnants, and ancient rock formations. It embraces more than 700 species, including Cayman's largest remaining contiguous ancient forest (one of the heavily deforested Caribbean's last examples). A comfortable walk depends on weather—winter is better because it's drier, though flowering plants such as the banana orchid blaze in summer. Call the National Trust to determine suitability and to book a guide ($24); tours run Tuesday through Friday morning by appointment. Or walk on the wild side with a $5 guidebook covering the ecosystems, endemic wildlife, seasonal changes, poisonous plants, and folkloric uses of flora. The trip takes about three hours. ✉ *Frank Sound Rd., East End ✛ Entrance by fire station at botanic park, Breakers* ☎ *345/749-1121, 345/749-1124 for guide reservations ⊕ www.nationaltrust.org.ky.*

HORSEBACK RIDING

Coral Stone Stables. Leisurely 90-minute horseback rides take in the white-sand beaches at Barkers and inland trails at Savannah; photos are included. Your guide is Noland Stewart, whose ranch contains 20 horses, chickens, and "randy" roosters. Nolan offers a nonstop narrative on flora, fauna, and history. He's an entertaining, endless font of local information, some of it unprintable. Rides are $75; swim rides cost $120. There's a $5 surcharge when paying by credit card. ✉ *Conch Point Rd., West Bay ✛ Next to*

Horseback riding in Barkers National Park

Ristorante Pappagallo on left ☎ *345/916–4799* ⊕ *www. coralstonestables.ky.*

Horseback in Paradise. Gregarious Nicki Eldemire loves telling stories about horse training and life on Cayman. She leads guided tours through Barkers National Park on the West End: an unspoiled peninsular area filled with enthralling plant and animal life along the beaches and wetlands. The steeper price (starting at $90) includes transportation, but it's a private, exclusive experience with no more than four riders per group. And the mounts—mostly Arabians, Paints, and Quarter Horses are magnificent. ⊠ *Barkers National Park, Conch Point, West Bay* ☎ *345/945–5839, 345/916–3530* ⊕ *www.caymanhorseriding.com.*

FAMILY **Pampered Ponies.** Offering "the ultimate tanning machine"— horses walking, trotting, and cantering along the beach— the stable leads private tours and guided trips, including sunset, moonlight, and bareback swim rides along the uninhabited beach from Conch Point to Morgan's Harbour on the north tip beyond West Bay. ⊠ *355 Conch Point Rd., West Bay* ☎ *345/945–2262, 345/916–2540* ⊕ *www.ponies.ky.*

KAYAKING

★ FodorsChoice **Cayman Kayaks.** Even beginners find the tours
FAMILY easy (the guides dub it low-impact aerobics), and the sit-
on-top tandem kayaks are stable and comfortable. The
Bio Bay tour involves more strenuous paddling, but the
underwater light show is magical as millions of bioluminescent microorganisms called dinoflagellates glow like
fireflies when disturbed. It runs only on moonless nights
and books well in advance. Passionate environmentalists, owners Tom and Lisha Watling, devised a way to
limit exposure of harmful repellent and sunscreen: they
designed a "black box" electric boat with a viewing
hole at the bottom, as well as high walls that focus your
glimpse of the stars above. Tours ($59–$69 with some
kids' and group discounts) depart from different locations, most from the public access jetty to the left of Rum
Point. They've temporarily discontinued the mangrove
wetlands tour, but it's a splendid learning experience when
it runs, providing an absorbing discussion of indigenous
animals (including a mesmerizing stop at a gently pulsing,
nonstinging Cassiopeia jellyfish pond) and plants, the
effects of hurricanes, and conservation efforts. ⊠ *Rum
Point Club, North Side, Rum Point* ☎ *345/746–3249,
345/926–4467* ⊕ *www.caymankayaks.com.*

SAILING

Though Cayman has a large sailing community, it isn't a
big charter-yacht destination. Still, you can skipper your
own craft (albeit sometimes under the watchful eye of the
boat's captain). The protected waters of the North Sound
are especially delightful, but chartering a sailboat is also a
wonderful way to discover lesser-known snorkeling, diving,
and fishing spots around the island.

SEA EXCURSIONS

The most impressive sights in the Cayman Islands are on
and under water, and several submarines, semisubmers-
ibles, glass-bottom boats, and Jules Verne–like contrap-
tions allow you to see these underwater wonders without
getting your feet wet. Sunset sails, dinner cruises, and
other theme (dance, booze, pirate) cruises are available
from $35–$90 per person.

FAMILY **Atlantis Submarines.** This submarine takes 48 passengers
safely and comfortably along the Cayman Wall down to 100

feet. Peep through panoramic portholes as good-natured guides keep up a humorous but informative patter. A guide dons scuba gear to feed fish that form a whirling frenzy of color rivaling anything by Picasso. At night, the 10,000-watt lights show the kaleidoscopic underwater colors and nocturnal stealth predators more brilliantly than during the day. Try to sit toward the front so you can watch the pilot's nimble maneuverings and the depth gauge. If that literally in-depth tour seems daunting, get up close and personal on the *Seaworld Observatory* semisubmersible (glorified glass-bottom boat), which just cruises the harbor (including glimpses of the *Cali* and *Balboa* shipwrecks). The cost is $104–$114 (children $49–$64) for the submarine, $44 (children $24) for the semisubmersible. There are frequent online booking discounts. ⌧ *30 S. Church St., George Town* ☎ *345/949–7700, 800/887–8571* ⊕ *www. caymanislandssubmarines.com.*

FAMILY **Jolly Roger.** This is a two-thirds-size replica of Christopher Columbus's 17th-century Spanish galleon *Niña.* (The company also owns the *Anne Bonny,* a wooden Norwegian brig built in 1934 that holds more than 100 passengers.) On the afternoon snorkel cruise, play Captain Jack Sparrow while experiencing swashbuckling pirate antics, including a trial, sword fight, and walking the plank; kids can fire the cannon, help hoist the main sail, and scrub the decks (they will love it even if they loathe doing chores at home). Evening options (sunset and dinner sails) are more standard booze cruises, less appropriate for the kiddies. Food is more appropriate to the brig, and it's more yo-ho-hokum than remotely authentic, but it's fun. Prices are $40–$59 (children's discounts available). ⌧ *South Terminal, next to Atlantis Submarines, George Town* ☎ *345/922–9922* ⊕ *www. jollyrogercayman.com, www.piratesofthecaymans.com.*

FAMILY **Sea Trek.** Helmet diving lets you walk and breathe 26 feet underwater for an hour—without getting your hair wet. No training or even swimming ability is required (ages eight and up), and you can wear glasses. Guides give a thorough safety briefing, and a sophisticated system of compressors and cylinders provides triple the amount of air necessary for normal breathing while a safety diver program ensures four levels of backup. The result at near-zero gravity resembles an exhilarating moonwalk ($89). ⌧ *Cayman Cabana, 53 N. Church St., George Town* ☎ *345/949–0008* ⊕ *www. seatrekcayman.com, www.snubacayman.com.*

6

SNORKELING

The proximity of healthy, Technicolor reef to the Grand Cayman shore means endless possibilities for snorkelers. Some sites require you to simply wade or swim into the surf; others are only accessible via boat. Nearly every snorkeling outfit follows the same route, beginning with the scintillating Stingray City and Sandbar. They usually continue to the adjacent Coral Gardens and often farther out along the Barrier Reef. Equipment is included, sometimes drinks, snacks, and lunch. Half-day tours run $35–$40, full-day $60–$75, and there are often extras such as kids' discounts and a complimentary shuttle to and from Seven Mile Beach resorts. Other popular trips combine Eden Rock, Cheeseburger Reef, and the wreck of the *Cali* off George Town. Most decent-size boats offer cover, but bring sunscreen and a hat.

SNORKELING SITES

★ Fodor's Choice **Stingray City Sandbar.** This site (as opposed to Stingray City, a popular 12-foot dive) is the island's stellar snorkeling attraction. Dozens of boats head here several times daily. It's less crowded on days with fewer cruise ships in port. ⊠ *North Sound.*

Wreck of the *Cali*. You can still identify the engines and winches of this old sailing freighter, which settled about 20 feet down. The sponges are particularly vivid, and tropical fish, shrimp, and lobster abound. Many operators based in George Town and Seven Mile Beach come here. ⊠ *93 N. Church St., George Town ✛ About 50 yards out from Rackam's Waterfront Pub.*

SNORKELING OPERATORS

Bayside Watersports. Offering half-day snorkel trips, North Sound beach lunch excursions, Stingray City and dinner cruises, and full-day deep-sea fishing, this company operates several popular boats out of West Bay's Morgan's Harbour. Full-day trips include lunch and conch diving November–April. ⊠ *Morgan's Harbour, West Bay* ☎ *345/928–2482* ⊕ *www.baysidewatersports.com.*

FAMILY **Captain Crosby's Watersports.** Offering favorably priced snorkeling ($40–$73 including refreshments) and dive excursions on well-equipped 47- and 40-foot trimarans, Captain Crosby is one of the more colorful captains in a group of genuine characters. He's actively involved in preserving Cayman's maritime heritage as a founder of the Catboat

CLOSE UP

Getting SASY

A few years ago, Wayne Hasson, a Cayman resident and owner of the live-aboard dive boat *Cayman Aggressor*, faced a dilemma. He and his wife, Anne, were both ardent, accomplished scuba divers and marine environmentalists. His children, then five and seven, understandably longed to share the diving experience, but their mother insisted that they simply snorkel atop the surface until they reached the age minimum of 12. They hated breathing in water and sputtering. So Hasson developed an ingenious compromise device that has already profoundly impacted the scuba industry and ocean education.

Hasson rigged a life vest with a pony bottle and regulator and let his kids try breathing from an air tank while positively buoyant at the surface. They remained face down without inhaling water, mimicking the feel of actual diving. The family worked on R&D for nearly a year with Custom Buoyancy, inventing and refining SASY (Supplied Air Snorkeling for Youth). The units resemble the real thing with life vest, small scuba tank (13 cubic feet as opposed to 19) in an adjustable holder, and regulator (all integrating crucial safety features like child-proof attachments and stabilizing straps); any kid five or older could now enjoy "diving" with Mom and Dad safely and comfortably. Recognizing adults might also feel awkward with snorkeling gear, Hasson created SASA (Supplied Air Snorkeling for Adults), which differs in the tank size (19 to 30 cubic feet). Although "snuba" allows you to go underwater, the hose can prove cumbersome and restrict the scope of your movement; kids as young as four can enjoy the feel of dive equipment with SASY, but the snuba minimum age is eight.

The device promotes interest in diving from a younger age, but equally important, the patent, trademarks, and income from sales and licensing agreements belong to Oceans for Youth, a nonprofit organization the Hassons subsequently founded to educate youth about the marine environment and the vital connection between sea and land life. As Hasson states, " ... the health of the world's oceans will soon become the responsibility of today's children."

6

Association. As a bonus, trips usually run a little long and often include a sing-along with the "singing captain." He also leads deep-sea fishing charters and gives sailing lessons ($150 per hour). ⊠ *Cayman Islands Yacht Club, Dock*

The waters on Stingray Sandbar are only about 3 to 4 feet deep.

C-29, Seven Mile Beach ☎ 345/945–4049, 345/916–1725 ⊕ *www.captaincrosbywatersports.com.*

FAMILY **Fantasea Tours.** Captain Dexter Ebanks runs tours on his 38-foot trimaran, *Don't Even Ask,* usually departing from the Cayman Islands Yacht Club ($40 including transfers). Tours are not too crowded (20 people max) and Ebanks is particularly helpful with first-timers. Like many captains, he has pet names for the rays (ask him to find Lucy, whom he "adopted") and rattles off factoids during an entertaining, nonstop narration. It's a laid-back trip, with Bob Marley and Norah Jones playing, fresh fruit and rum punch on tap. ⊠ *West Bay Rd., Seven Mile Beach* ☎ *345/916–0754* ⊕ *www.dexters-fantaseatours.com.*

FAMILY **Red Sail Sports.** Luxurious 62- and 65-foot catamarans (the *Spirits of Cayman, Poseidon, Calypso,* and *Ppalu*) often carry large groups on Stingray City, sunset, and evening sails ($45–$85, $22.50–$42.50 children under 12) including dinner in winter. Although the service may not be personal, it's efficient. A glass-bottom boat takes passengers to Stingray City/Sandbar and nearby coral reefs. Trips run from several hotels, including the Westin and Morritt's, in addition to the Rum Point headquarters. ☎ *345/949–8745, 345/623–5965, 877/506–6368* ⊕ *www.redsailcayman.com.*

CLOSE UP

Stingray City

Hundreds of gray and khaki Atlantic southern stingrays, resembling inquisitive alien life forms, enact an acrobatic aqua-ballet as they circle this North Sound site seeking handouts from divers and snorkelers. The area actually encompasses two separate locations: Stingray City, called by many the world's greatest 12-foot dive, and the nearby sandbar, where people can wade in waist-deep water.

Steve Irwin's tragic demise rekindled humankind's age-old fear of these beautiful, mysterious "devil" creatures with their barbed tails. The Atlantic southern stingrays are a different, smaller species than the stingray that killed Irwin and as close to tame as possible. Shy and unaggressive by nature, they use their tails only in defense; nonetheless, don't pick rays up unless you follow your guide's careful instructions.

Stingray City's origins can be traced to local fishermen who would moor inside the fringe reef, then clean their catch, tossing the scraps overboard. Captain Marvin Ebanks, who still runs trips in his 90s, recalls feeding them as a child. The rays, who hunt via keen smell (and sensitive electroreceptors stippling their underside, near the mouth), realized they'd discovered their own restaurant and began hanging around. They slowly became inured to human interaction, rarely displaying the species' typical timidity. They glide like graceful giants (up to 4 feet in diameter), practically nuzzling you with their silken bellies, begging petlike for food. Indeed, crews recognize them (and vice versa), fondly giving the rays nicknames (Hoo-Ray, X-Ray, Gamma Ray), insisting they have distinct personalities.

Instead of teeth, their mouths contain viselike sucking grips. Keep your palms face-up and as flat as possible so they don't unintentionally "swallow" your fingers (their eyes are located atop their bodies, so they hover over and practically hoover your hand in excitement).

More formal visitation guidelines have now been established because 5 to 20 boats visit twice daily, and the population is growing at an alarming rate. Feeding is restricted to appointed tour operators; only natural bait fish like ballyhoo and squid are permitted; the food amount is limited; and any remains and litter must be removed. Many Caymanians and divers oppose altered feeding because it changes the ecosystem's natural food chain. But some concede the good outweighs the bad: The interaction is magical, not to mention fostering greater appreciation and environmental awareness.

6

SQUASH AND TENNIS

Most resorts and condominium complexes have their own courts, often lighted for night play, but guests have top priority. When empty, you can book a court, which normally costs around $25 per hour.

WINDSURFING AND KITEBOARDING

The East End's reef-protected shallows extend for miles, offering ideal blustery conditions (15 to 35 mph in winter, 6- to 10-knot southerlies in summer) for windsurfing and kiteboarding. Boarders claim only rank amateurs will "tea-bag" (kite-speak for skidding in and out of the water) in those "nuking" winds. They also rarely "Hindenburg" (stall due to lack of breeze) off West Bay's Palmetto Point and Conch Point.

CAYMAN BRAC

Updated
by Jordan
Simon

CAYMAN BRAC IS NAMED FOR its most distinctive feature—a moody, craggy limestone bluff (*brac* in the Gaelic
of the Scottish highlands fishermen who settled the islands
in the 18th century) that runs up the spine of the 12-mile
(19-km) island, culminating in a sheer 140-foot cliff at its
eastern end, the country's highest and easternmost point.
The bluff holds the angry Atlantic at bay, gradually taper-
ing like a coil losing its spring in the west. Nature's artistry—and awesome power—is also evident in the many
caves and sinkholes that stipple the crag, long rumored
to hold pirates' gold. The islandscape is by far the most
dramatic in the Cayman Islands, though divers the world
over come for the spectacular underwater topography and
sponge-encrusted wrecks.

The Brac, as it's commonly called, sits 90 miles (143 km)
northeast of Grand Cayman, accessible only via Cayman
Airways (and private boat), but it's nothing like the cosmopolitan and Americanized Grand Cayman. With only
2,100 residents—they call themselves Brackers—the island
has the feel and easy pace of a small town. Brackers are
known for their friendly attitude toward visitors, so it's
easy to strike up a conversation. You're never treated like a
stranger; locals wave when they pass and might invite you
home for a traditional rundown (a thick, sultry fish stew)
and storytelling, usually about the sea, the turtle schooners,
and the great hurricane of 1932 (when the caves offered
shelter to islanders). Brackers are as calm and peaceful as
their island is rugged, having been violently sculpted by
sea and wind, most recently by Hurricane Paloma, which
leveled the island in November 2008 (locals quip that all
18 churches sustained significant damage—but no bars).

Columbus first discovered the island by mistake during
his final voyage in 1503; explorers and privateers made
infrequent pit stops over the next three centuries, the Bluff
serving as a vital navigational landmark. Though the Brac
wasn't permanently settled until the 1830s, its short history
seethes with dramatic incident, from marauding pirates to
ravaging hurricanes. Today, despite its small size (roughly
12 miles by 1½ miles [19 km by 2 ½ km], or 14 square miles
[36 square km]), the Brac is reinventing itself as an ecocentric adventure destination. Aside from diving, bonefish in
the shallows and game fish in the deeper offshore waters
lure anglers. The island hosts numerous ecosystems from
arid semidesert stippled with cacti to ancient dry woodlands thick with exotic, fragrant flowers and trees. More

than 200 bird species, both indigenous and migratory—including the endangered Cayman Brac parrot—flutter about. Nature trails filigree the interior, and several caves can be easily accessed. No surprise that the island is also considered one of the world's most exotic rock-climbing destinations, famous for its sheer vertical cliffs.

Hamlets with names like Watering Place, Cotton Tree Bay, Creek (Rock), and Spot Bay hold charming restored homes typical of seafaring architecture embroidered with carefully tended yards bursting with tropical blooms. Dozens of tiny churches line the road, bordered by sand graveyards. Despite the expats gradually boosting the year-round population, development remains as blissfully slow as the pace, though one longtime escapee from the stateside rat race grumbles about fancier cars and faster driving. There's still no stoplight, and traffic is defined by two locals stopping in the middle of the road to chat. It's as idyllic as a partially developed island can be. Indeed, the Brac is the affectionate butt of jokes from other Caymanians: "Two 60-year-old Brackers were so bored they decided to put in a bomb threat," starts one; the punch line is that they fall asleep first. Another refers to the three or four families dominating the phone book: "The most confusing day of the year on the Brac is Father's Day."

ORIENTATION

The island is easy to navigate. One main road hugs the north coast, another the south, while a paved roller-coaster bypass (Ashton Reid Drive) across the Bluff roughly bisects the island, linking the two sides. Numerous gravel and dirt roads crisscross the island, but these are best avoided. The main hotel development and nicest beaches lie near the airport in the West End (the island's lowest point, at sea level). The southern road climbs the Bluff, passing spectacular caves and cliffs, ending at the Parrot Reserve and Lighthouse, with their splendid panoramic trails. The north road accesses the tiny towns of Stake Bay and Spot Bay, where several historic attractions are located.

PLANNING

WHEN TO GO

The Brac is sleepy year-round, and there's less of a difference in price between low and high season than on other islands, as diving, climbing, and fishing can be experienced throughout the year, as does bird-watching (though winter

TOP EXPERIENCES

■ **Diving.** Cayman Brac is unquestionably one of the world's great scuba destinations, from walls and wrecks exploding with kaleidoscopic marine life to wondrous man-made creations like the "Lost City of Atlantis" underwater installation.

■ **Lighthouse Walk.** In addition to thrilling Caribbean vistas and an eerie, almost lonely lunar look, you experience nature's fierce elemental savagery, the crescendo of crashing surf and whipping wind.

■ **Local Crafts.** Several "old timer" artisans keep

traditions alive. Visiting their shops (often in their homes) is a marvelous immersion in Bracker culture.

■ **Caving.** Several caves are accessible—most easily, some via a mildly strenuous hike; in addition to striking natural formations, they played a vital role in sheltering islanders during storms.

■ **Museum-hop.** The Cayman Brac Museum pays tribute to this remote island's maritime tradition; though small, it's jam-packed with odd, often poignant little artifacts.

attracts the migrant fowl). Some properties close for maintenance in September during hurricane season, and prices are generally lower in summer.

GETTING HERE AND AROUND

AIR TRAVEL

Cayman Airways Express provides Twin Otter service several times daily from Grand Cayman to Cayman Brac. There's also direct service from Miami on larger aircraft. Depending on the flight route, you may land on Little Cayman first. The flight is approximately 40 minutes nonstop. Cayman Brac has its own small airport, Sir Captain Charles Kirkconnell International Airport (CYB).

CAR TRAVEL

You need a car to really explore Cayman Brac, though hotels often provide complimentary bikes. Your own valid driver's license is necessary to obtain a temporary local driving permit ($20), which can be used on any of the Cayman Islands. Rental cars range from $35 to $55 per day depending on the type and size of the vehicle.

Driving is on the left. Gasoline is expensive; there are only two stations (one at each end of the island), and hours can be erratic. The main road circumnavigating the island and the bypass over the Bluff connecting the north and south coasts are well maintained. Yellow lines on roads indicate no parking zones. Most locals park on the side of the road.

Four D's, which carries mostly Nissans, tends to have cheaper rates, but rarely offers discounts. B&S Motor Ventures offers compacts, midsize vehicles, jeeps, SUVs, and vans. The only on-site airport agency, CB Rent-A-Car, has Honda, Hyundai, and Toyota vehicles, from compact cars to minivans. Most agencies offer a low-season discount and/or complimentary pickup and drop-off.

Contacts B&S Motor Ventures. ☎ 345/948–1646 ⊕ www.bandsmv. com. **CB Rent-A-Car.** ✉ Airport Dr., Gerrard Smith Airport, West End ☎ 345/948–2424, 345/948–2847 ⊕ www.cbrentacar.com. **Four D's Car Rental.** ☎ 345/948–1599, 345/948–0459.

TAXI TRAVEL
Brackers often wear several hats, so your tour guide might also take you out fishing or serve you drinks; all of them are fonts of local lore and legend. An island day tour generally costs $25 per person, with a minimum of two people. Occasionally, you may have to wait to be picked up. Your hotel can arrange airport transfers. Rates are generally fixed: $8 to the closest hotels like Cayman Brac Beach Resort, $15 to Cayman Breakers near the southeastern tip, $20 to the Bight and Spot Bay on the north side. Drivers will generally load up passengers from several properties, including individual villas.

The tourist office and the hotels have a list of preferred providers, all Brackers who can regale you with stories of their upbringing.

VISITOR INFORMATION
From 8:30 to 5 pm on weekdays, the affable staff at the Sister Islands office of the Cayman Islands Department of Tourism can supply brochures on accommodations, dive outfits, activities, and nature and heritage trails. This office also services Little Cayman.

Contacts Cayman Islands Department of Tourism. ✉ 209 West End Community Park, West End ☎ 345/948–1649 ⊕ www.cayman-islands.ky, itsyourstoexplore.com.

RESTAURANTS

Most resorts offer optional meal plans, but there are several independent restaurants on the island, some of which provide free transport from your hotel. Local restaurants serve island fare (local seafood, chicken, and curries, as well as addictive beef patties). On Friday and Saturday nights the spicy scent of jerk chicken fills the air; several roadside stands sell take-out dinners. Look for the local specialty, a sweetish, pillow-soft, round bread.

HOTELS

Lodgings are small and intimate, and guests are often treated like family, congregating in the lobby or bar to swap stories, tall or otherwise, of their exploits. There are only a few full-service resorts, two of them condo complexes. There are also a couple of cozy guesthouses and several private villas (usually second homes for snowbirds) for rent throughout the island. In November 2008, Hurricane Paloma wiped out most of the island's larger properties. All have been rebuilt, in some cases from the ground up.

WHAT IT COSTS IN U.S. DOLLARS			
	$	$$	$$$	$$$$
Restaurants	under $12	$12–$20	$21–$30	over $30
Hotels	under $275	$275–$375	$376–$475	over $475

Prices in the restaurant reviews are the average cost of a main course at dinner or, if dinner is not served, at lunch; taxes and service charges are generally included. Prices in the hotel reviews are the lowest cost of a standard double room in high season, excluding taxes, service charges, and meal plans (except at all-inclusives). Prices for rentals are the lowest per-night cost for a one-bedroom unit in high season.

EXPLORING CAYMAN BRAC

The Brac abounds in both natural and historic attractions. Many of the former include botanic gardens and preserves set aside to protect threatened indigenous species. The latter revolve around the maritime heritage and hardscrabble lives of the earliest settlers and their descendants up until the island developed better communication with the outside world in the 1970s. *For more specific listings of caves and nature trails of particular significance, see Sports and the Outdoors.*

If you're exploring on your own, be sure to pick up the *Cayman Brac Heritage Sites & Trails* brochure, available at the tourist office and most hotels; it lists all the major points of interest.

The **Sister Islands District Administration** (☎ *345/948–2222, ask for organizer Chevala Burke* ⊕*www.naturecayman. com*) offers free government-sponsored guided nature and cultural tours with trained local guides Cantrell Scott and Keino Daley. Options include the Parrot Reserve, nature trails, wetlands, Lighthouse/Bluff View, caving, birding, and heritage sites.

WHAT TO SEE

Cayman Brac Museum. A diverse, well-displayed collection of historic Bracker implements ranges from dental pliers to pistols to pottery. A meticulously crafted scale model of the Caymanian catboat *Alsons* has pride of place. The front room reconstructs the Customs, Treasury, bank, and post office as they looked decades ago. Permanent exhibits include those on the 1932 hurricane, turtling, shipbuilding, and old-time home life. The back room hosts rotating exhibits such as one on herbal folk medicine. ⊠ *Old Government Administration Bldg., Stake Bay* ☎*345/948–2622, 345/244–4446* ☜*Free.*

Heritage House. An acre of beautifully landscaped grounds dotted with thatched gazebos and fountains includes an old-fashioned well and tannery as well as Cola Cave (used to shelter the former estate owners during hurricanes), with informational panels. The main building, though new, replicates a traditional house; the interior has a few displays and videos depicting Brac history, but the most fascinating element is watching local artists at work. It's a great resource for books on natural history and Caymanian crafts. Daily slide shows, various cultural events, and talks by visiting naturalists are often scheduled. Call before visiting to make sure that the house is open. ⊠ *218 North East Bay Rd., Spot Bay* ☎*345/948–0563* ☜*Free.*

★ Fodor'sChoice **Parrot Preserve.** The likeliest place to spot the endangered Cayman Brac parrot—and other indigenous and migratory birds—is along this National Trust hiking trail off Major Donald Drive, aka Lighthouse Road. Prime time is early morning or late afternoon; most of the day they're camouflaged by trees, earning them the moniker "stealth parrot." The loop trail incorporates part of a path

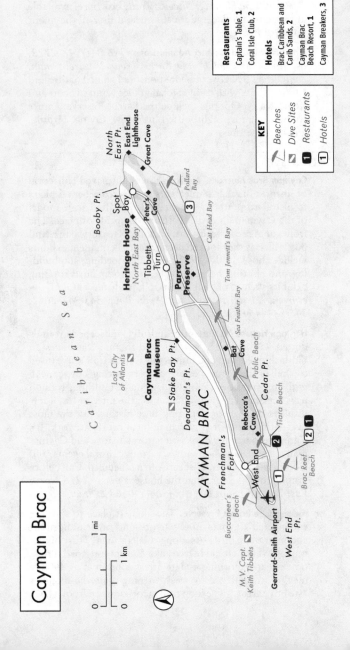

Cayman Brac

Caribbean Sea

Restaurants
Captain's Table, **1**
Coral Isle Club, **2**

Hotels
Brac Caribbean and
Carib Sands, **2**
Cayman Brac
Beach Resort, **1**
Cayman Breakers, **3**

KEY
↗ Beaches
◪ Dive Sites
1 Restaurants
1 Hotels

North East Pt.
East End Pt.
East End
Lighthouse
Great Cave
Pollard Bay
Booby Pt.
Spot Bay
Peter's Cave
3
Cat Head Bay
Heritage House
North East Bay
Tibbetts Turn
Parrot Preserve
Tom Jennett's Bay
Sea Feather Bay
Cayman Brac Museum
◪ Stake Bay Pt.
Bat Cave
Public Beach
Cedar Pt.
Tiara Beach
Deadman's Pt.
CAYMAN BRAC
Lost City of Atlantis
Rebecca's Cave
2
Frenchman's Fort
West End
1
2 1
Brac Reef Beach
Buccaneer's Beach
Gerrard-Smith Airport
West End Pt.
M.V. Capt. Keith Tibbets ◪

0 ——— 1 mi
0 ——— 1 km

the Brackers used in olden days to cross the bluff to reach their provision grounds on the south shore or to gather coconuts, once a major export crop. It passes through several types of terrain: old farmland under grass and native trees from mango to mahogany unusually mixed with orchids and cacti. Wear sturdy shoes, as the terrain is rocky, uneven, and occasionally rough. The 6-mile (10-km) gravel road continues to the lighthouse at the bluff's eastern end, where there's an astonishing view from atop the cliff to the open ocean—the best place to watch the sunrise. ⊠ *Lighthouse Rd., Tibbetts Turn* ✛ *½ mi (1 km) south of town* ☎ *345/948–0319* ⌖ *Free*.

THE GREAT HURRICANE OF '32. Brackers were ill prepared for hurricanes, especially the deadly storm with 200 mph winds that blustered its way over the island in 1932, destroying virtually everything in its path. Most Brackers took shelter in the caves sculpted from the Bluff. Others flooded into the Spellman-McLaughlin home, which miraculously stood fast, saving 130 people. A "tear of sea" (archaic argot for a tidal wave) crashed onto shore, sending a boulder hurtling through the front door. Other than some damage from flooding, the house withstood the brunt of the storm, and even the windows remained unbroken. Even younger Brackers still discuss the storm with awe, though Paloma matched its fury.

WHERE TO EAT

$$ ✕ **Captain's Table.** *European.* This weathered, powder-blue, wooden building wouldn't be out of place on some remote New England shore, except perhaps for the garish pirate at the entrance. The nautical yo-ho-hokum continues inside—painted oars, model sailboats, faux portholes, a mermaid painting, and droll touches like a skeleton with a chef's toque. **Known for:** "honey-stung" chicken; shoot the breeze with locals and dive crew; nautical decor. ⑤ *Average main: $19* ⊠ *Brac Caribbean, 165 South Side Rd.* ☎ *345/948–1418*.

$$ ✕ **Coral Isle Club.** *Caribbean.* This seaside eatery daubed in a virtual rainbow of blues from turquoise to teal serves up fine local food, emphasizing fresh seafood and, on weekends, mouth- and eye-watering barbecue. The lusciously painted outdoor bar offers equally colorful sunsets, cocktails, and characters (one regular swears, "If I were any

better, I'd be dangerous," before buying another round).
Known for: fun local clientele; mouthwatering barbecue;
weekend entertainment. $ *Average main: $18* ✉ *Off South
Side Rd., West End* ☎ *345/925–4848.*

WHERE TO STAY

Cayman Brac currently has just one full-scale resort, as
well as several apartments. Several private villas on Cayman Brac can also be rented, most of them basic but well
maintained, ranging from one to four bedrooms. The rental
fees are quite reasonable, and normally the price for extra
couples in the larger units is only $200 per week (singles
$100–$135, children often free), representing substantial
savings for families or couples traveling together, while
the kitchen helps reduce the price of dining out. In addition, government tax and often a service fee are sometimes
included in the quoted rate (be sure to verify this), and
most villa owners arrange a 10% discount with car-rental
agencies. As a general rule of thumb, properties are thoroughly cleaned before your arrival; you must pay extra if
you want daily maid service, and a one-time cleaning fee
of $50 to $75 is usually assessed for end-of-rental cleaning. Owners can sometimes arrange to stock the fridge
before your arrival. Each villa has a manager who must
meet you at the airport (or car-rental agency), then escort
you to your home; you'll be provided with his or her contact information during the reservation process. Rates are
sometimes discounted in the off-season. Contact the tourist
office for information.

Most villa owners mandate a three- to seven-night minimum stay in high season (assume at least one week's booking during the Christmas holiday unless otherwise noted),
though this is often negotiable. Some owners will leave a
kayak or snorkeling gear out for guests' use. If such amenities are included, they're mentioned. Unless otherwise
noted, properties have landlines; local calls are usually
free, but phones are generally locked for international
calls. If your GSM provider works in the Cayman Islands,
activate the international capability, but note that service
is poor or nonexistent at some villas on the south side
beneath the Bluff.

*Hotel reviews have been shortened. For full information,
visit Fodors.com.*

$ ▣ **Brac Caribbean and Carib Sands.** *Resort.* These neighboring, beachfront sister complexes offer condos with one to four bedrooms, all individually owned and decorated. **Pros:** lively restaurant-bar; weekly discounts excellent value for families; reasonably priced for beachfront property. **Cons:** narrow unmaintained beach; limited staff; Wi-Fi dodgy. ⑤ *Rooms from: $190* ✉ *Bert Marson Dr.* ☎ *345/948–2265, 866/843–2722, 345/948–1121, 864/498–4206 toll-free* ⊕ *www.caribsands.com, www.866thebrac.com* ⇌ *65 condos* ⊘ *No meals.*

$$ ▣ **Cayman Brac Beach Resort.** *Resort.* Popular with divers, this well-run eco-friendly resort, completely renovated in 2015–16, features a beautiful sandy beach shaded by sea grape trees slung with hammocks and a sizable free-form pool. **Pros:** great dive outfit; friendly vibe; free Wi-Fi; good online packages; coin-operated laundry. **Cons:** noise from planes; view often obscured from ground-floor units; mandatory airport transfer of $20 per person. ⑤ *Rooms from: $317* ✉ *West End* ☎ *345/948–1323, 727/308–7474 for reservations in Florida, 855/484–0808* ⊕ *www.caymanbracbeachresort.com* ⇌ *40 rooms* ⊘ *Some meals.*

$ ▣ **Cayman Breakers.** *Rental.* This attractive, pink-brick, colonnaded condo development sitting between the bluff and the southeast coastal ironshore caters to climbers, who scale the bluff's sheer face, as well as divers, who appreciate the good shore diving right off the property. **Pros:** spectacular views; thoughtful extras like complimentary bikes, jigsaw puzzles, and climbing-route guides; very attentive managers who live on-site. **Cons:** nearest grocery is a 15-minute drive; gorgeous beach is rocky with rough surf; some units slightly musty and faded. ⑤ *Rooms from: $175* ✉ *The Moorings, 1902 South Side Rd. E, near East End* ☎ *345/948–1463, 345/927–8826* ⊕ *www.caymancondosonline.com* ⇌ *26 2-bedroom condos* ⊘ *No meals.*

BEACHES

Much of the Brac's coastline is ironshore, though there are several pretty sand beaches, mostly along the southwest coast (where swimmers will also find extensive beds of turtle grass, which creates less than ideal conditions for snorkeling). In addition to the hotel beaches, where everyone is welcome, there is a public beach with good access to the reef; it's well marked on tourist maps. The north-coast beaches, predominantly rocky ironshore, offer excellent snorkeling.

Pollard Bay. The beach by Cayman Breakers is fairly wide for this eastern stretch of the island. Start clambering east underneath the imposing bluff, past the end of the paved road, to strikingly beautiful deserted stretches accessible only on foot. The water here starts churning like a washing machine and becomes progressively rockier, littered with driftwood. Locals search for whelks here. Steps by the Breakers lead to shore dive sites. Flocks of seabirds darken the sun for seconds at a time, while blowholes spout as if answering migrant humpback whales. Don't go beyond the gargantuan rock called First Cay—the sudden swells can be hazardous—unless you're a serious rock climber. **Amenities:** none. **Best for:** solitude; walking. ⊠ *South Side Rd. E, East End.*

Public Beach. Roughly 2 miles (3 km) east of the Brac Reef and Carib Sands/Brac Caribbean resorts, just past the wetlands (the unsightly gate is visible from the road; if you hit the Bat Cave you've passed it), lie a series of strands culminating in this beach, relatively deserted despite its name. The surf is calm and the crystalline water fairly protected for swimming. There are picnic tables and showers in uncertain condition. Snorkeling is quite good. **Amenities:** showers. **Best for:** snorkeling. ⊠ *South Side Rd. W.*

Sea Feather Bay. The central section of the south coast features several lengthy ribbons of soft ecru sand, only occasionally maintained, with little shade aside from the odd coconut palm, no facilities, and blissful privacy (aside from some villas). **Amenities:** none. **Best for:** solitude; swimming, walking. ⊠ *South Side Rd., just west of Ashton Reid Dr., Sea Feather Bay.*

SPORTS AND THE OUTDOORS

BIRD-WATCHING

Bird-watching is sensational on the Sister Islands, with almost 200 species patrolling the island from migratory to endemic, including the endangered Cayman Brac parrot and brown booby. The best place to spy the feathered lovelies is on the north coast and in the protected woodland reserve *(see Parrot Reserve in Exploring Cayman Brac)* on the Bluff. Other species to look out for include the indigenous vitelline warbler and red-legged thrush. The wetlands and ponds in the West End teem with herons and shorebirds, including splendid frigates, kestrels, ospreys, and rare West

House of Worship

The pale blue, circular Temple Beth Shalom nestles incongruously in the Waltons' serene garden, replete with the only consecrated Jewish cemetery in the Cayman Islands. A plaque by the imposing carved mahogany door reads "House of Welcome, May All Who Enter Here Find Peace." Brooklyn-born Lynne presides over services, though rabbis and cantors fly in for special occasions and holidays. George erected the synagogue as a gift to his wife but says, "I hope that any person from around the world will talk to God as they understand Him without intervention. ... Protestants love the temple; they spend more time here than the Jews, even one of the most hard-core Baptist families we have." Indeed, visitors from Argentina to Austria to Australia have renewed their spirits here.

Swiss architect Fredy Schulteiss designed the building, but George and Lynne practically built it by themselves. It includes stained glass, Italian marble accents from Italy, and polished gray Minnesota granite floors they laid themselves. Lynne carved everything from the marble to the Honduran mahogany doors and inlaid scrolling fashioned from dead limbs of wild plum, cedar, mahogany, ironwood, and candlewood trees. Her father created a menorah in the shape of a shofar; another was a family heirloom brought by Lynne's grandmother from Odessa. The synagogue is actually one structure encased within another, "one for the Torah, the other to reach toward the heavens, in a small way making a statement to God that we're trying to get there." The 28-foot ceiling fittingly depicts a starry sky, with the 12 lights representing the 12 tribes of Israel. As a bonus, the space has splendid acoustics and a piano. Members of the Cayman National Orchestra, including flutists, pianists, and cellists, occasionally perform memorable classical concerts.

Indian whistling ducks. Most coastal areas offer sightings, but the best may be just inland at the **Westerly Ponds** (which connect during rainy season; otherwise boardwalks provide excellent viewing areas). A hundred species flap about, particularly around the easternmost pond off Bert Marson Drive by Mr. Billy's house: the old Bracker feeds them late afternoon and occasionally early morning, when the whistling ducks practically coat the entire surface of the water.

A diver swimming between coral formations

DIVING AND SNORKELING

Cayman Brac's waters are celebrated for their rich diversity of sea life, from hammerhead and reef sharks to stingrays to sea horses. Divers and snorkelers alike will find towering coral heads, impressive walls, and fascinating wrecks. The snorkeling and shore diving off the **north coast** are spectacular, particularly at West End, where nearby coral formations attract all kinds of critters. The walls feature remarkable topography with natural gullies, caves, and fissures blanketed with Technicolor sponges, black coral, gorgonians, and sea fans. Some of the famed sites are the West Chute, Cemetery Wall, Airport Wall, and Garden Eel Wall.

The **South Wall** is a wonderland of sheer drop-offs carved with a maze of vertical swim-throughs, tunnels, arches, and grottoes that divers nickname Cayman's Grand Canyon. Notable sites include Anchor Wall, Rock Monster Chimney, and the Wilderness.

Notable diving attractions around the island include the 330-foot MV *Capt. Keith Tibbetts,* a Russian frigate purchased from Cuba and deliberately scuttled in 1996 within swimming distance of the northwest shore, accessible to divers of all levels. Many fish have colonized the Russian frigate—now broken in two and encrusted with magnificent orange and yellow sponges. Other underwater wrecks include the *Cayman Mariner,* a steel tugboat, and the *Prince*

Frederick, a wooden-hulled twin-masted schooner that allegedly sank in the 19th century.

Oceanic Voyagers, a 7-foot-tall bronze statue created by world-renowned marine sculptor Dale Evers, depicts spotted dolphins cavorting with southern stingrays. It was sunk off the Brac's coast near Stake Bay in January 2003 as part of the Cayman Islands' yearlong quincentennial celebration. An artist named Foots has created an amazing underwater Atlantis off Radar Reef.

Other top snorkeling/shore diving spots include the south coast's **Pillar Coral Reef, Tarpon Reef,** and **Lighthouse Reef;** the north shore counters with **Greenhouse Reef, Snapper Reef,** and **Jan's Reef.**

Brac Scuba Shack. Partners Martin van der Touw, wife Liesel, and Steve Reese form a tremendous troika at this PADI outfit, whose selling points include small groups (10 divers max on the custom Newton 36), flexible departures, valet service, and computer profiles. The 30-foot central console *Big Blue* takes no more than five divers and does double-duty for deep-sea fishing. Courses range from Discover Scuba through Divemaster Training, as well as such specialties as wreck, nitrox, and night diving. Rates are par for the course ($110 for two-tank dives), but multiday discounts are available. ⊠ *West End* ☎ *345/948–8472, 345/925–3215 mobile* ⊕ *www.bracscubashack.com.*

Reef Divers. Pluses here include five Newton boats from 42 to 46 feet, valet service, and enthusiastic, experienced staff; slightly higher rates reflect the extras. Certified divers can purchase à la carte dive packages even if they aren't hotel guests. They also arrange snorkeling tours. ⊠ *Cayman Brac Beach Resort, West End* ☎ *345/948–1642, 345/948–1323* ⊕ *www.reefdiverscaymanbrac.com, www. caymanbracbeachresort.com.*

FISHING

Cayman Brac offers superior bonefishing along the shallows off the southwest coast and even finer light-tackle action. The offshore waters mostly compose a marine park, so fishers go out a few hundred feet from the dive buoys, themselves ranging ¼ to ½ mile (½ to 1 km) from shore. The pristine environment teems with wahoo, marlin, and sushi-grade tuna. Most charter-boat operators also run snorkeling trips; a memorable excursion is to Little Cayman Brac, passing several fanciful rock formations.

HIKING

Public footpaths and hiking trails filigree the island, with interpretive signs identifying a staggering variety of resident and nonresident bird species that call the Brac home. You'll also find reptile habitats, indigenous flora, and historically and geologically significant sites. Arguably the most scenic route traverses the eastern Bluff to the tip, where the remains of a lighthouse stand sentinel over the roaring Caribbean. This is one of the routes taken by early Brackers scaling the Bluff via the steep **Lighthouse Steps** up past Peter's Cave *(see Spelunking)*, then down the 2½-mile (4-km) **Lighthouse Footpath** adjacent to Major Donald Drive (aka Lighthouse Road). This was used to bring cattle to pasture, as well as to access plantations of cassava, peppers, beans, tomatoes, sweet potatoes, mangoes, bananas, and other crops. The panoramas are awe inspiring, especially once you reach the lighthouse. Even though the path along the edge is fairly even, it's not suitable for the elderly, very young, or infirm due to high winds (don't venture onto the dramatic bleached limestone outcroppings: a sudden gust could send you hurtling into the air with the brown boobies that nest in ledges and caves here). It's a compellingly desolate, eerie area, as if future spacefarers were terra-forming the moon with hardy "maypole" cacti, century plants, aloes, and wind-lashed silver thatch palms bowing almost as if in deference to nature.

Brac Tourism Office. Free printed guides to the Brac's many heritage and nature trails can be obtained here (and from the airport and hotels). Traditional routes across the bluff have been marked, as are trailheads along the road. It's safe to hike on your own, though some trails are fairly hard going (wear light hiking boots) and others could be better maintained. ⊠ *West End Community Park, west of airport* ☎ *345/948–1649* ⊕ *www.itsyourstoexplore.com.*

Christopher Columbus Gardens. For those who prefer less-strenuous walking, these gardens have easy trails and boardwalks. The park showcases the unique natural flora and features of the bluff, including two cave mouths. This is a peaceful spot dotted with gazebos and wooden bridges comprising several ecosystems from cacti to mahogany trees. ⊠ *Ashton Reid Dr. (Bluff Rd.), just north of Ashton Rutty Centre.*

CLOSE UP

Sculpting Cayman

A Brac sculptor known as Foots (real name Ronald Kynes) for his size-16 feet, dreamed of re-creating Plato's lost city of Atlantis. Four decades later, he realized this dream by creating mammoth sculptures and sinking them 45 feet off the Brac's north shore. The resulting artificial reef is an astounding artistic achievement and an engineering feat with more than 100 pieces covering several acres; even partial destruction by Hurricane Paloma didn't faze Foots.

An architect-contractor fascinated by ruins and mythology, Foots found his niche restoring historic buildings, including churches in Germany, Austria, and Iran. To secure permits, he submitted a video of his ideal site and a 140-page environmental impact report to the Department of the Environment, noting the goodwill and revenue it would generate in the scuba and tourism industries. "I have money, I just need your blessing," Foots wrote.

He has spent thousands of dollars ("What price making a dream come true?") and years of his life into the project, which launched officially in 2005, when 150,000 pounds of sculpture were submerged. Specially constructed barges helped position the pieces by cranes, lift bags, and drag floats. The technical marvel encompasses nearly 300,000 pounds. The scale is immense, but, as Foots says, "Hopes and dreams make the world livable ... I'm promoting new life and marine growth through art that will last an eternity."

The story starts at the Archway of Atlantis (its two bases weigh 21,000 pounds each). The Elders' Way, lined with 5-foot temple columns, leads to the Inner Circle of Light, centering a 2,600-pound sundial. Two 50,000-pound pyramids tower 20 feet with eight swim-throughs. One ambitious project, the Colossus, a toppled 30-foot statue broken into pieces like 7-foot-long feet and a scepter, will suggest the Lost City's destruction.

Foots modeled the statues after actual people who have contributed to Cayman. He fashions exact plaster of paris molds of their faces (and sometimes hands), then casts in limestone-based cement. Copper piping and doorknobs ingeniously replicate papyrus scrolls; apothecary bottles complete the Medicine Men.

The project has continually evolved inside Foots's head since childhood, without architectural renderings: "I invent so many phases I'd never live long enough to finish ... Atlantis will only end when I do."

7

Sister Islands District Administration. The administration arranges free, government-sponsored, guided nature and cultural tours with trained local guides. Options include the Parrot Reserve, nature trails, wetlands, Lighthouse/Bluff View, caving, birding, and heritage sites. ☎ *345/948–2222.*

ROCK CLIMBING

Aficionados consider the Brac among the world's leading exotic climbing destinations. If you are experienced and like dangling from ropes 140 feet above a rocky, churning sea, this is the place for you. Unfortunately, if you want to learn the ropes, no organization promotes climbing, though a new service rents equipment such as ropes and safety gear. Through the years, climbers have attached permanent titanium bolts to the **Bluff** face, creating some 70 routes in seven prime regions around the East End, most notably the Spot Bay areas, the North Wall, the East Wall, and the South Wall. Access is often via private property, so be respectful (though most Brackers will just invite you in for cold drinks and stimulating conversation). The number is still growing as aficionados create new ascents. Difficulty is high; the "easiest" routes are graded 5.8 by the Yosemite Decimal System; most are rated 5.10 to 5.12, though many experienced climbers argue some approach the dizzying 5.14 range, especially around the sheer, "pumpy" (rock-speak for adrenaline-flowing) Northeast Point. This is steep, gnarly terrain of varying stability, suitable only for experienced climbers. Most of the Bluff's faces are hard vertical to overhanging; many walls vault abruptly to the savage sea.

Climbing the Brac is exhilarating, but precautions are vital. Sturdy hiking boots are mandatory, since you'll traverse a wide variety of terrain just accessing routes. Leather gloves are also recommended, as most of the high-quality limestone is smooth but has sharp and jagged areas. Two ropes are necessary for many climbs, the longest of which requires 19 quickdraws. Gear should include ascending devices like prusiks and Tiblocs and shoulder-length slings with carabiners. Don't attempt climbs alone. Establish rope tug signals, as the wind, waves, and overhangs make hearing difficult. Always analyze surf conditions and prevailing winds (which are variable) before rappelling, and double-check rap setup, anchors, and harnesses. Though titanium glue-ins replaced most of the old stainless steel bolts, many are deteriorating due to stress corrosion cracking; avoid any old bolts.

The Cayman Breakers condo complex has route maps and descriptions *(see Where to Stay)*. Several world-renowned climbers have built (second) homes on the Brac, including Liz Grenard, John Byrnes, and Ian Stewart.

READ ABOUT THE BRAC. Ian Stewart wrote a fine article on Brac climbing for the website of the Sister Islands Department of Tourism (⊕ www.caymanbrac.com/islandattractions/climbing. html). The J. W. Harper blog also contains useful links (⊕ www. skipharper.com). Though some of these articles and trip reports were written a few years ago, they're still pertinent. A more regularly updated blog devoted to the destination is ⊕ www. climbcaymanbrac.com.

Rock Iguana. This company, run by world-class climbers, operates out of a mobile van, taking aficionados and amateurs alike to the Brac's best sites. They offer both instruction and top-notch gear (they've also been upgrading the bolts around the island). Rock Iguana can accommodate most requests, whether your thrill is rappelling down a sheer rock face or squeezing through barely accessible caverns carved into the bluff. Tours begin at $145 per person; instruction for all levels is $450 for two intense days. ✉ *Mobile van* ☎ *345/936–2722* ⊕ *climb.ky*.

SPELUNKING

Residents and geologists are still discovering "new" caves and sinkholes in the Brac's 25- to 30-million-year-old dolomite rock. Most of these caves were formed when the sea receded after the last Ice Age. Rainwater dissolved the carbonate rock over millennia through cracks made by plants rooting in the limestone. Mineral deposits fashioned fanciful formations in many caves, as well as more typical pillars, stalagmites, and daggerlike stalactites.

Buccaneers (supposedly including Henry Morgan and Edward "Blackbeard" Teach) of the 17th and 18th centuries stopped like most mariners at the Cayman Islands to restock stores of water, wood, and turtles. Many locals still believe buried treasure lies deep within the recesses of the Bluff. But more vitally, the caves served as shelter during the fearsome storms of the first part of the 20th century.

Most caves are closed to the public—even to experienced spelunkers—but several are easily accessed and considered safe. If you plan to explore Cayman Brac's caves, wear good

sneakers or hiking shoes, as some paths are steep and rocky and some entrances reachable only by ladders.

Peter's Cave offers a stunning aerial view of the picturesque northeastern community of Spot Bay. The climb is easier from atop the Bluff; the other access is steep, and purchase isn't always easy even with railings. The chambers feature few formations but some pretty multihue striations. **Great Cave,** at the island's southeast end, has numerous chambers and photogenic ocean views. It's the least accessible yet most impressive. You won't fund Bruce Wayne or his Boy Wonder in the **Bat Cave,** but you may see Jamaican fruit bats hanging from the ceiling (try not to disturb them), as well as nesting barn owls. The bats play a crucial role in the ecosystem's food chain because they devour overripe fruits, thereby pollinating plants, disseminating seeds, and reducing insect pests. There are some whimsical formations, and sections cracked and crawling with undergrowth, trees, and epiphytes. **Rebecca's Cave** houses the graveside of an 18-month-old child who died during the horrific hurricane of 1932. A plaque commemorates her short life ("Daughter of Raib and Helena 'Miss Missy' Bodden"), and people still leave flowers. It's actually a ¼-mile (½-km) hike inland along a well-marked trail called the Saltwater Pond Path, which continues to the north side. Today it's a prime bird-watching walk lined with indigenous flora like red birch, jasmine, silver thatch palms, agave, dildo cactus, balsam, cabbage trees, duppy bushes, and bull hoof plants.

CAYMANITE. Found only in the crevices of the Bluff, this stone is actually an amalgam of several metals and minerals, including magnesium, iron, calcium, sodium, copper, nickel, phosphorus, and more—practically a quarter of the periodic table. Its striations supposedly represent different geologic eras, ranging from russet to white; no two pieces are identical. Special tools including diamond-tipped cutting wheels and grinders hone the extremely hard rock to a dazzling marble-like finish.

Thatch Weaving

"Laying rope" is an old-time tradition that originated so that women could support themselves while the men were away at sea, often for months at a time. The Brac was particularly noted for the method of stripping silver thatch palm leaves and drying them in the sun, both creating a labor-intensive twisted hemplike rope that was exported to Jamaica, usually in barter, and various baskets for carrying sand (for gardens) and provisions from little farms atop the Bluff.

You can visit the home studio/shop of the craft's foremost practitioner, **Annelee Ebanks** (*35 White Bay Rd., West End, 345/948–1326*), whose skill is such that the Ritz-Carlton commissions her to create pieces as gifts, decorative accents, towel hampers, and waste baskets. Miss Annelee began more than half a century ago at 13 watching her father make traditional baskets. She "decided as the years went on to start new patterns. I dream at night, sketch the idea, then go back to sleep."

The stripped dried thatch "strings" have several gradations in hue from silvery mint to buff; bunches are tied off in places to ensure the sun doesn't bleach out all the color. She also uses darker brown dried stripped coconut leaves to create multicolored pieces: place mats with matching coasters and napkin rings, hats, baskets, purses, sandals, hand fans, even brooms and switches ("for bad boys"), since thatching originally served utilitarian purposes. It takes her three days to create one beach bag: one day to weave, a second to line and stitch, another to decorate (she uses Magic Marker and spray paint, as well as raffia from Jamaica for binding and decorative curlicues).

Amazingly nimble, she'll gladly demonstrate the process but might recruit you if you prove adept. A bunch (usually two to eight strands) is tied at the bottom; use the thumb and index finger to hold and weave, pleating in and out. "Bend and crease it good at the bottom, then you be the boss of it."

7

SHOPPING

Shopping is limited on the Brac; there are a few small stores, though many locals sell their wares from home. You'll also find a boutique at the Cayman Brac Beach Resort. Specialty crafts here are woven-thatch items and Caymanite jewelry.

★ **Fodor's**Choice **NIM Things.** Artist and raconteur Tenson Scott fashions exquisite jewelry from Caymanite (he climbs down from the lighthouse without ropes to chisel the stone), triton shells, sea eggs, and more unusual materials—hence the name, which stands for Native Island Made. His wife, Starrie, creates delicate works from sea urchins, hardening the shell with epoxy: cute turtles, bud vases, and planters decorated with minuscule shells. ⊠ *North East Bay Rd., Spot Bay* ☎ *345/948–0461, 345/939–5306.*

NIGHTLIFE

Divers are notoriously early risers, but a few bars keep things hopping if not quite happening, especially on weekends, when local bands (or "imports" from Grand Cayman) often perform. Quaintly reminiscent of *Footloose* (without the hellfire and brimstone), watering holes are required to obtain music and dancing permits. Various community events including talent shows, recitals, concerts, and other stage presentations at the Aston Rutty Centre provide the rest of the island's nightlife.

Barracuda's Bar. New Yorker Terry Chesnard built his dream bar from scratch, endowing it with an almost 1960s Rat Pack ambience. Nearly everything is handcrafted, from the elegant bar itself to the blown-glass light fixtures to the drinks. Try the Barracuda shot special "if you dare," or the cocktails, though Terry takes the greatest pride in his top-of-the-line espresso machine. The kitchen elevates pub grub to an art form with pizzas, Reubens, and French melts. Locals flock here for free pasta Fridays, karaoke Wednesdays, and live music on Thursdays. You might walk in on a hotly contested darts, shuffleboard, or dominoes tournament, but the vibe is otherwise mellow at this charming time-warp hangout. ⊠ *20 West End Rd., Creek* ☎ *345/948–8511.*

Tipsy Turtle Pub. This pub overflows with good cheer and strong drinks. The mudslides are particularly potent, and there are usually some good Cubanos. The alfresco, split-level bar (great water views from the top) serves excellent pub grub (jerk chicken pizza, Caesar salad wrap, portobello-and-Swiss cheeseburger, messy and marvelous spare ribs, tempura shrimp) for around $10 a dish. It's the kind of casual congenial hangout where almost everyone ends up buying a round at some point. Stop by for Tuesday bingo, Wednesday karaoke, or Friday barbecue with live music, which attracts large, enthusiastic crowds. ⊠ *Cayman Brac Beach Resort, West End* ☎ *345/948–1323.*

LITTLE CAYMAN

8

Updated
by Jordan
Simon

THE SMALLEST AND MOST TRANQUIL of the three inhabited Cayman Islands, Little Cayman has a full-time population of only 170, most of whom work in the tourism industry; they are easily outnumbered by iguanas and rare birds. This 12-square-mile (31-square-km) island is practically pristine and has only a sand-sealed airstrip, sharing its "terminal" building with the fire department and a few other vehicles. The grass runway was finally paved with blacktop a few years ago, and locals no longer have to line up their cars at night to guide emergency landings in by headlight. But some things don't change. The speed limit remains 25 mph, as no one is in a hurry to go anywhere. In fact, the island's population of resident iguanas uses roads more regularly than residents; signs created by local artists read "Iguanas have the right of way."

With little commercial development, the island beckons ecotourists seeking wildlife encounters, not urban wild life. It's best known for its spectacular diving in world-renowned Bloody Bay Marine Park, including Bloody Bay Wall and adjacent Jackson Wall. The ravishing reefs and plummeting walls encircling the island teem with more than 500 different species of fish and more than 150 kinds of coral. Fly-, lake-, and deep-sea fishing are also popular, as well as snorkeling, kayaking, and biking. And the island's certainly for the birds. The National Trust Booby Pond Nature Reserve is a designated wetland of international importance, which protects around 20,000 red-footed boobies, the Western Hemisphere's largest colony. It's just one of many superlative spots to witness avian aerial acrobatics.

Secluded beaches, unspoiled tropical wilderness and wetlands, mangrove swamps, lagoons, bejeweled coral reefs—Little Cayman practically redefines "hideaway" and "escape." Yet aficionados appreciate that the low-key lifestyle doesn't mean sacrificing the high-tech amenities, and some of the resorts cater to a quietly wealthy yet unpretentious crowd.

Which isn't to say Little Cayman lacks for lively moments. Halloween parties and Mardi Gras festivities bring out wildly imaginative costumes and floats. It's just one of those rare places that attract more colorful types who are in search of privacy, not just the ardently ecocentric.

TOP EXPERIENCES

■ **Wall-to-Wall Fun.** Divers can't miss the hallowed Bloody Bay, lauded by every Cousteau worth his sea salt.

■ **Bird-Watching.** Even if you're not a birder, learning about the rare red-footed booby from its fanatics at the National Trust and spying them through telescopes are more fun than you'd think.

■ **Beachcombing.** A jaunt to Owen Island or Point of Sand rewards you with practically virgin strands, breathtaking views, and scintillating snorkeling.

■ **Something Fishy.** The deep-sea fishing is superior, but the light-tackle option should lure any angler.

ORIENTATION

Little Cayman is bracketed by lighthouses at the West and East Ends, whose terrain couldn't be more different. The semiarid East End has a remote, end-of-the-world feel: Limestone sinkholes called karst stitched with xeric shrub give it a pitted moonlike appearance. The West End is much greener. But beaches, snorkeling, nature trails, and bird-viewing areas embroider the entire island. One main road, mostly paved, essentially circumnavigates the coast. Several packed-dirt side roads crisscross the island, often accessing the more remote beaches. These can become muddy and almost impassable in heavy rain.

8

PLANNING

WHEN TO GO

Though diving and fishing excel in summer as well, the traditional high-season months of December through April apply to Little Cayman, as they do to hotels in much of the Caribbean. Most of the small resorts shut down September through most of October, during the height of hurricane season.

GETTING HERE AND AROUND

AIR TRAVEL

Interisland service between Grand Cayman, Cayman Brac, and Little Cayman is provided several times daily by Cayman Airways at Edward Bodden Airfield, which accommodates only STOL craft.

CAR TRAVEL

Bikes, usually offered for free by the resorts, are the preferred way of getting around the island; dive operations
will pick you up, and the hotels also provide airport
transfers. A car is suggested only if you rent one of the
more isolated villas or if you plan to explore the farther-flung part of the island on a regular basis. Parking
is rarely a problem. Another flexible touring option is a
moped. Little Cayman Car Rental offers mopeds ($50)
and SUVs ($80–$100). There are also two scooter companies offering competitive rates.

Information Little Cayman Car Rental. ☎ *345/948–1000* ✍ *lit-*
tlcay@candw.ky. **Scoot Around Little Cayman.** ☎ *345/924–6229,*
345/916–0656. **Scooten! Scooters!** ☎ *345/916–4971* ⊕ *www.*
scootenscooters.com.

TAXI TRAVEL

Resorts offer airport transfers. Two companies offer land
tours (in addition to fishing, kayaking, and other options).
Island tours are usually $50 per person (though each addi-
tional person is generally discounted, as are children). LCB
Tours has a safari bus for larger groups. Maxine McCoy's
MAM's Tours can accommodate up to 15 passengers in
two minivans, though she's often off-island.

Information LCB Tours. ✉ *Little Cayman Beach Resort, Blossom*
Village ☎ *345/948–1642, 345/948–1033.* **MAM's Tours.** ✉ *65 Ma-*
hogany Bay, Candle Rd., West End ☎ *345/948–0104, 345/917–4582*
mobile ⊕ *www.mams.ky.*

RESTAURANTS

The main resorts' dining rooms accept reservations from
nonguests pending availability. Otherwise, there are two
full-fledged restaurants, both affiliated with villa/condo
properties. The choices are limited, with seafood obviously
reigning supreme, but the caliber of the few kitchens is
generally high.

HOTELS

Accommodations are mostly in small lodges, almost
all of which offer meal and dive packages. The chefs in
most places create wonderful meals despite often-limited
resources. You won't find any independent restaurants,
but if you are staying in a villa or condo you can usually
have dinner at one of the resorts (be sure to call ahead).
Dive packages represent exceptional savings. Most resorts
prefer a five- to seven-night stay in high season, but the

minimum isn't always strictly enforced. Still, rooms for shorter stays may not become available until two to three weeks prior to your trip dates.

WHAT IT COSTS IN U.S. DOLLARS				
	$	**$$**	**$$$**	**$$$$**
Restaurants	under $12	$12–$20	$21–$30	over $30
Hotels	under $275	$275–$375	$376–$475	over $475

Prices in the restaurant reviews are the average cost of a main course at dinner or, if dinner is not served, at lunch; taxes and service charges are generally included. Prices in the hotel reviews are the lowest cost of a standard double room in high season, excluding taxes, service charges, and meal plans (except at all-inclusives). Prices for rentals are the lowest per-night cost for a one-bedroom unit in high season.

VISITOR INFORMATION

There is no visitor center on Little Cayman, but each hotel, hotelier, and staffer overflows with information and suggestions. You can also consult the websites of the **Sister Islands Tourism Association** (⊕ *www.itsyourstoexplore.com*) for information on Little Cayman.

EXPLORING LITTLE CAYMAN

Little Cayman isn't much for man-made sights and attractions; those that are here essentially serve to explain and promote nature preserved in all her finery, especially underwater, throughout the island. If you're exploring on your own, pick up the *Little Cayman Heritage Sites and Trails* brochure, available at the hotels and National Trust; it lists all the major points of interest.

EXPLORING

★ Fodor'sChoice **Gladys B. Howard Little Cayman National Trust Visitors Centre.** This traditional Caymanian cottage overlooks the Booby Pond Nature Reserve; telescopes on the breezy second-floor deck permit close-up views of their markings and nests, as well as other feathered friends. Inside are shell collections; panels and dioramas discussing endemic reptiles; models "in flight"; and diagrams on the growth and life span of red-footed boobies, frigate birds, egrets, and other island "residents." The shop sells exquisite jewelry made from Caymanite and spider-crab shells, extraordinary duck decoys and driftwood carvings, and great books on history, ornithology, and geology. Mike Vallee holds an

Little Cayman

KEY

- Beaches
- Dive Sites
- **1** Restaurants
- **1** Hotels

Restaurants

Hungry Iguana, **2**
Pirates Point, **1**

Hotels

The Club, **4**
Little Cayman Beach Resort, **3**
Paradise Villas, **2**
Pirates Point Resort, **1**
Southern Cross Club, **5**

Caribbean Sea

LITTLE CAYMAN

EASTERN BLUFF

Jackson Wall

Bloody Bay Wall

Bloody Bay

Spot Bay

Anchorage Bay

West End Lighthouse
West End Pt.

Westerly Ponds

Preston Bay

Edward Bodden Airfield

South Town

Little Cayman Museum

Blossom Village Park

Jacksons Pt.

Little Cayman Research Centre

Booby Pond Nature Reserve

Booby Pond

Grape Tree Bay

Lower Spot Bay

Tarpon Lake

Wearis Bay

Gladys B. Howard Little Cayman National Trust Visitors Centre

Owen Island

Charles Bight

Crawl Bay

Mary's Bay

Charles Bight Pond

Snipe Pt.

East Pt.

Point of Sand

Rosetta Flats

0   1 mi

0   1 km

iguana information session and tour every Friday at 4. The cheeky movie *Calendar Girls* inspired a local equivalent: women from Little Cayman going topless for an important cause—raising awareness of the red-footed booby and funds to purchase the sanctuary's land. Nicknamed, appropriately, "Support the Boobies," the calendar is tasteful, not titillating: the lasses strategically hold conch shells, brochures, flippers, tree branches, etc. ⊠ *Blossom Village* ⊕ *www.nationaltrust.org.ky.*

Little Cayman Museum. This gorgeously laid out and curated museum displays relics and artifacts, including one wing devoted to maritime memorabilia and another to superlative avian and marine photographs, which provide a good overview of this tiny island's history and heritage. ⊠ *Across from Booby Pond Nature Reserve, Blossom Village* ☎ *345/323–7166* ⊠ *Free.*

Little Cayman Research Center. Near the Jackson Point Bloody Bay Marine Park reserve, this vital research center supports visiting students and researchers, with a long list of projects studying the biodiversity, human impact, reef health, and ocean ecosystem of Little Cayman. Reefs this unspoiled are usually far less accessible; the National Oceanic and Atmospheric Administration awarded it one of 16 monitoring stations worldwide. The center also solicits funding through the parent U.S. nonprofit organization Central Caribbean Marine Institute; if you value the health of our reefs, show your support on the website. Chairman Peter Hillenbrand proudly calls it the "Ritz-Carlton of marine research facilities, which often are little more than pitched tents on a beach." Tours explain the center's mission and ecosensitive design (including Peter's Potty, an off-the-grid bathroom facility using compostable toilets that recycle fertilizer into gray water for the gardens); sometimes you'll get a peek at the upstairs functional wet labs and dormitories. To make it layperson-friendlier, scientists occasionally give talks and presentations. The Dive with a Researcher program (where you actually help survey and assess environmental impact and ecosystem health, depending on that week's focus) is hugely popular. ⊠ *North Side* ☎ *345/948–1094* ⊕ *www.reefresearch.org.*

8

WHERE TO EAT

$$$ ✕**Hungry Iguana.** *Eclectic.* The closest thing to a genuine sports bar and nightclub on Little Cayman, the Iggy caters to the aquatically minded set with a marine mural, wood-plank floors, mounted trophy sailfish, lots of fishing caps, and yummy fresh seafood. Conch fritters are near definitive, while lionfish fingers with jerk mayo are mouth- and eye-watering. ⑤ *Average main: $26* ⊠ *Paradise Villas, Guy Banks Rd., Blossom Village* ☎ *345/948–0007* ⊕ *www.paradisevillas.com* ⊘ *No dinner Sun.*

★ Fodor'sChoice ✕**Pirates Point.** *Eclectic.* Susan Howard continues
$$$$ the tradition of her mother (the beloved late, irrepressible Gladys Howard), offering Texas-style and Texas-size hospitality at her ravishing little resort. Guests have first privilege, but the kitchen can usually accommodate an extra couple or two. **Known for:** jovial atmosphere; fine dining; popular sushi nights. ⑤ *Average main: $40* ⊠ *Pirates Point Resort, Preston Bay* ☎ *345/948–1010* ⊕ *www.piratespointresort.com* ⊘ *Closed Sept.–mid-Oct. No lunch.*

WHERE TO STAY

Accommodations are mostly in small lodges, many of which offer meal and dive packages. The meal packages are a good idea; the chefs in most places create wonderful dishes with often limited resources.

Hotel reviews have been shortened. For full information, visit Fodors.com.

PRIVATE VILLAS

A few private villas on Little Cayman can be rented, most of them basic but well maintained, ranging from one to four bedrooms. There are also three condo complexes and one villa resort on the island. Rental fees are reasonable, and normally the price for extra couples in the larger units is only $200 per week, representing substantial savings for families or couples traveling together, while the kitchen helps reduce the price of dining out. In addition, government tax and often a service fee are sometimes included in the quoted rate (be sure to verify this). As a general rule of thumb, properties are thoroughly cleaned before your arrival; you must pay extra if you want daily maid service. Rates are sometimes discounted in the off-season. Most villa owners mandate a three- to seven-night minimum stay in high season, though this is often negotiable. Unless

CLOSE UP

Iggin Out

An estimated 2,000 prehistoric-looking Little Cayman rock iguanas roam the island, by far the largest population in Cayman. The late Gladys Howard, former chair of the Little Cayman committee of the nonprofit National Trust for the Cayman Islands, took the good fight for the boobies and applied it to the "iggies." Visitors can feed these large (up to 5 feet), fierce-looking but docile vegetarians by hand at the residential Mahogany Bay neighborhood, where the crea-tures' preferred delicacies—fruit trees and flowers from bananas and papayas to hibiscus—flourish. But Gladys's cohorts hope to purchase more coastal land to serve as a nesting sanctuary. She knew it's a crucial component of ecotourism and, noting how the same species has all but disappeared on the Brac (while the blue iguana still faces extinction on Grand Cayman), said, "We want to avoid that fate. We must preserve them because so few of that species remain on our planet."

otherwise noted, properties have landline phones; local calls are usually free, but phones are generally locked for international calls.

RECOMMENDED HOTELS AND RESORTS

$$ ☷**The Club.** *Rental.* These ultramodern, luxurious, three-bedroom condos are Little Cayman's nicest units, though only five are usually included in the rental pool. **Pros:** luxurious digs; lovely beach; hot tub. **Cons:** housekeeping not included; rear guest bedrooms dark and somewhat cramped; handsome but heavy old-fashioned decor. ⑤ *Rooms from: $311* ⊠ *South Hole Sound* ☎ *345/948–1033, 727/323–8727, 888/756–7400* ⊕ *www.theclubatlittlecayman.com* ⤳ *8 condos* ⏃○⏃ *No meals.*

$$$ ☷**Little Cayman Beach Resort.** *Resort.* This two-story hotel, **FAMILY** the island's largest, offers modern facilities in a boutique setting. **Pros:** extensive facilities; fun crowd; glorious LED-lit pool; great bone- and deep-sea fishing. **Cons:** less intimate than other resorts; tiny patios; bike rental fee. ⑤ *Rooms from: $434* ⊠ *Blossom Village* ☎ *345/948–1033, 855/485–0022 toll-free* ⊕ *www.littlecayman.com* ⤳ *40 rooms* ⏃○⏃ *Some meals.*

$ ☷**Paradise Villas.** *Rental.* Cozy, sunny, one-bedroom units with beachfront terraces and hammocks are simply but immaculately appointed with rattan furnishings, marine

8

Pirates Point Resort

artwork, painted driftwood, and bright abstract fabrics.
Pros: friendly staff; good value, especially online deals and
dive packages. **Cons:** noisy some weekend nights in season; poky beach; small bike rental fee; off-site dive shop.
⑤ *Rooms from: $229* ⊠ *South Hole Sound* ☎ *345/948–0001,
877/322–9626* ⊕ *www.paradisevillas.com* ☉ *Closed mid-Sept.–late Oct.* ➷ *12 1-bedroom villas* ⑩ *No meals.*

★ Fodor'sChoice ☆ **Pirates Point Resort.** *Resort.* Comfortable rooms
$$$$ and fine cuisine make this hideaway nestled between sea
grape and casuarina pines on a sweep of sand one of Little Cayman's best properties. **Pros:** fabulous food; fantastic beach; dynamic dive program; fun-loving staff and
owner. **Cons:** tasteful rooms are fairly spare; occasional
Internet problems. ⑤ *Rooms from: $500* ⊠ *Pirates Point*
☎ *345/948–1010* ⊕ *www.piratespointresort.com* ☉ *Closed
Sept.–mid-Oct.* ➷ *11 rooms* ⑩ *All-inclusive.*

★ Fodor'sChoice ☆ **Southern Cross Club.** *Resort.* Little Cayman's first
$$$$ resort was founded in the 1950s as a private fishing club by
the CEO of Sears-Roebuck and CFO of General Motors, and
its focus is still on fishing and diving. **Pros:** barefoot luxury;
free use of kayaks and snorkel gear; splendiferous beach;
international staff tells of globe-trotting exploits. **Cons:** not
child-friendly (though families can rent a cottage); Wi-Fi not
available in some rooms and spotty elsewhere. ⑤ *Rooms from:
$748* ⊠ *South Hole Sound* ☎ *345/948–1099, 800/899–2582*
⊕ *www.southerncrossclub.com* ☉ *Closed mid-Sept.–mid-Oct.*
➷ *12 suites, 1 2-bedroom cottage* ⑩ *All meals.*

CLOSE UP

Art Dive

The bar at Pirates Point typifies the fun, funky sensibility of the dive set, who adorn their favorite resorts with painted stones and driftwood. Here you'll find an idiosyncratic, imaginative gallery of mobiles, painted sandals, coconut fronds, and found art. An old oar fashioned into the likeness of a Caymanian lizard might read "Texas Roadkill Dive Club"; sculpted penguins say "We don't know how we got here but we know we're not leaving." The late founder Gladys Howard created an annual competition for best creation, with prizes including free stays. The staff provides brushes, paints, and a hot-glue gun; guests canvas for raw materials on the shore. One recent winner was a lionfish created from palm fronds and sea sponges.

BEACHES

The southwest part of the island seems like one giant beach; this is where virtually all the resorts sit, serenely facing Preston Bay and South Hole Sound. But there are several other unspoiled, usually deserted strands that beckon beachcombers, all the sand having the same delicate hue of Cristal Champagne and just as apt to make you feel giddy.

Blossom Village Park. Developed by the local chapter of the National Trust, the site of the first, albeit temporary, Cayman Islands settlement, in the 1660s, is lined with traditional cottages. Bricks are dedicated to old-time residents and longtime repeat guests. There are picnic tables, a playground, and a dock. The beach is small but has plenty of shade trees, good snorkeling, and calm water. **Amenities:** none. **Best for:** snorkeling, swimming.

★ Fodor'sChoice **Owen Island.** This private, forested island can be reached by rowboat, kayak, or an ambitious 200-yard swim. Anyone is welcome to come across and enjoy the deserted beaches and excellent snorkeling as well as fly-fishing. Nudity is forbidden as "idle and disorderly" in the Cayman Islands, though that doesn't always stop skinny-dippers (who may not realize they can be seen quite easily from shore). **Amenities:** none. **Best for:** fishing, snorkeling; solitude; swimming.

★ Fodor'sChoice **Point of Sand.** Stretching over a mile on the island's easternmost point, this secluded beach is great for

8

Southern Cross Club

wading, shell collecting, and snorkeling. On a clear day you can see 7 miles (11 km) to Cayman Brac. The beach serves as a green- and loggerhead turtle nesting site in spring, and a mosaic of coral gardens blooms just offshore. It's magical, especially at moonrise, when it earns its nickname, Lovers' Beach. There's a palapa for shade but no facilities. The current can be strong, so watch the kids carefully. **Amenities:** none. **Best for:** snorkeling; solitude; sunset; walking.

SPORTS AND THE OUTDOORS

Little Cayman is a recreational paradise on land and especially underwater, with world-class diving, light-tackle angling, and bird-watching the star attractions. Befitting an ecocentric destination, nature owns the island, and you're strictly cautioned about dos and don'ts. But lectures are given with a smile, and then you're free to explore this zoo without cages, and aquarium without tanks.

BIRD-WATCHING

Little Cayman offers bountiful bird-watching, with more than 200 indigenous and migrant species on vibrant display, including red-footed boobies, frigate birds, and West Indian whistling ducks. Unspoiled wetland blankets more than 40% of the island, and elevated viewing platforms (carefully crafted from local wood to blend harmoniously with the environment) permit undisturbed observation—but then, it's hard to find an area that doesn't host flocks of warblers and waterfowl. Brochures with maps are available at the hotels for self-guided bird-watching tours.

★ Fodor'sChoice **Booby Pond Nature Reserve.** The reserve is home to 20,000 red-footed boobies (the Western Hemisphere's largest colony) and Cayman's only breeding colony of magnificent frigate (man-of-war) birds. Other sightings include the near-threatened West Indian whistling duck and vitelline warbler. The RAMSAR Convention, an international treaty for wetland conservation, designated the reserve a wetland of global significance. Near the airport, the sanctuary also has a gift shop and reading library. ✉ *Next to National Trust, Blossom Village.*

National Trust. The website of the National Trust and the Sister Islands Tourism Authority has information on bird-watching. ⊕ *www.itsyourstoexplore.com, www.nationaltrust.org.ky.*

BIRD-WATCHING SITES

★ Fodor'sChoice **Tarpon Lake.** There's more here than just fishing. A long deck extends into the writhing tangle of red mangrove roots, where white herons, ospreys, and whistling ducks dive-bomb for fiddler crabs and mosquito fish skittering through the brackish water alongside sun-silvered pirouetting tarpon. ✉ *Off Guy Banks Rd.*

8

DIVING AND SNORKELING

A gaudy tumble of marine life—lumbering grouper to fleet guppies, massive manta rays to miniature wrasse, sharks to stingrays, blue chromis to Bermuda chubs, puffers to parrotfish—parades its finery through the pyrotechnic coral reefs like a watery Main Street on Saturday night. Gaping gorges, vaulting pinnacles, plunging walls, chutes, arches, and vertical chimneys create a virtual underwater city, festooned with fiery sponges and gorgonians draped over limestone settees.

Expect to pay around $105–$110 for a two-tank boat dive and $25–$30 for a snorkeling trip. The island is small and susceptible to wind, so itineraries can change like a sudden gust.

Bloody Bay Wall

DIVE AND SNORKEL SITES

Snorkelers will delight in taking Nancy's Cup of Tea or "scaling" Mike's Mountain, as well as enjoying Eagle Ray Roundup, Three Fathom Wall, and Owen Island. The areas around the East End are difficult to access from shore due to the jagged ironshore (boats are often preferable) but are worthwhile: Mary's Bay, Snipe Point, and Lighthouse Reef (which has stunning Brac vistas).

Among the many superlative dive sites are the Great Wall, the Meadows, the Zoo, Coconut Walk Wall, School Bus Stop, Sarah's Set, Black Hole, Mixing Bowl, Charlie's Chimneys, and Blacktip Boulevard.

★ Fodor'sChoice **Bloody Bay Wall.** This beach, named for being the site of a spectacular 17th-century sea battle, was declared one of the world's top three dive sites by the *maîtres* Jacques and Philippe Cousteau. Part of a protected marine reserve, it plunges dramatically from 18 to 6,000 feet, with a series of staggeringly beautiful drop-offs and remarkable visibility. Snorkelers who are strong swimmers can access the edge from shore, gliding among shimmering silver curtains of minnows, jacks, and bonefish. The creatures are amazingly friendly, including Jerry the Grouper, whom dive masters joke is a representative of the Cayman Islands Department of Tourism.

★ Fodor'sChoice **Jackson Wall.** Adjacent to Bloody Bay, Jackson Wall and reef are nearly as stunning. Conditions are variable, the water now glassy, now turbulent, so snorkelers must be strong swimmers. It's renowned for Swiss-cheese-like swim-throughs; though it's not as precipitous as Bloody Bay, the more rugged bottom results in astonishing rock formations whose tunnels and crevices hold pyrotechnic marine life.

RECOMMENDED OPERATORS

Pirates Point Dive Resort. This popular resort has fully outfitted 42-foot Newtons with dive masters who excel at finding odd and rare creatures, and encourage computer diving so you can stay down longer. ⊠ *Pirates Point Resort* ☎ *345/948–1010* ⊕ *www.piratespointresort.com.*

Reef Divers. Little Cayman Beach Resort's outfitter offers valet service and a full complement of courses, with nitrox a specialty. The custom boats include AEDs (defibrillators). ⊠ *Little Cayman Beach Resort, Blossom Village* ☎ *345/948–1033* ⊕ *www.littlecayman.com.*

Southern Cross Club. Each boat (spanking new Newtons added in 2017) has its own dock and takes 12 divers max. The outfit has good specialty courses and mandates computer diving. ⊠ *Southern Cross Club, 73 Guy Banks Rd., South Hole Sound* ☎ *345/948–1099, 800/899–2582* ⊕ *www. southerncrossclub.com.*

FISHING

Bloody Bay is equally celebrated for fishing and diving, and the flats and shallows including South Hole Sound Lagoon across from Owen Island, Tarpon Lake, and the Charles Bight Rosetta Flats offer phenomenal light-tackle and fly-fishing action: surprisingly large tarpon, small bonefish, and permit (a large fish related to pompano) weighing up to 35 pounds. Superior deep-sea fishing is available right offshore for game fish including blue marlin, dolphin, wahoo, tuna, and barracuda.

★ Fodor'sChoice **Southern Cross Club.** The resort offers light-tackle and deep-sea fishing trips with a knowledgeable, enthusiastic staff (book in advance, even as a hotel guest). There's even a skiff with a poling tower to spot the more elusive fish. ⊠ *Southern Cross Club, 73 Guy Banks Dr., South Hole Sound* ☎ *345/948–1099, 800/899–2582* ⊕ *www.southerncrossclub.com.*

HIKING

Flat Little Cayman is better suited to biking, but there are a few jaunts, notably the **Salt Rocks Nature Trail**, where you pass ancient mule pens, abandoned phosphate mines, and the rusting tracks of the original narrow-gauge railway now alive with a profusion of flowering cacti and scrub brush.

TRAVEL SMART
CAYMAN ISLANDS

GETTING HERE AND AROUND

Grand Cayman is a relatively small island, and the longest distance you can travel should take no more than a couple of hours. You can get by on Grand Cayman using a combination of tours and local buses (especially if you are staying in the Seven Mile Beach area), but if you want to explore on your own, it's easier with a rental car. Although driving is on the left, British style, Grand Cayman's well-paved road system makes independent travel fairly easy, though signage is not always clear. Cayman Brac and Little Cayman are even tinier and can be navigated by bike or moped.

▌ AIR TRAVEL

Several carriers offer frequent nonstop or direct flights between North America and Grand Cayman's Owen Roberts Airport. Flying time from New York is about four hours, just over an hour from Miami. Only small STOL propeller aircraft serve Cayman Brac and Little Cayman.

AIRPORTS

Grand Cayman's Owen Roberts Airport (GCM) is a modern facility located in the western, busier section of the island, roughly 2 miles (3 km) east of George Town. The current multimillion-dollar expansion and general upgrade (to meet the projected increase in arrivals over the next two decades) should be completed by late 2019. The airport is about 15 minutes from

hotels situated along Seven Mile Beach, about 30 to 45 minutes from the East End and West Bay lodgings, and 10 minutes from George Town. Cayman Brac's Sir Captain Charles Kirkconnell Airport (CYB) can accommodate smaller jets, while Little Cayman's Edward Bodden Airstrip can only accommodate prop aircraft due to runway limitations.

Airport Information Edward Bodden Airstrip (LYB). ☎ 345/948–0021. **Owen Roberts International Airport (GCM).** ☎ 345/943–7070. **Sir Captain Charles Kirkconnell International Airport (CYB).** ☎ 345/948–1222.

GROUND TRANSPORTATION

In Grand Cayman, ground transportation is available immediately outside the customs area of the airport. Taxis aren't metered, but fares are government-regulated (about $15–$30 to resorts along Seven Mile Beach, $60 to the East End). Be sure, however, to confirm the fare before getting into the taxi and whether the price quoted is in U.S. or Cayman dollars.

Round-trip airport transfers are generally included (or at least offered) by hotels on the Sister Islands, where most accommodations sit within 10 minutes' drive of the airports.

Taxis are always available at Grand Cayman's airport. They don't dependably meet flights on the

Sister Islands, so make sure your resort or villa company has made arrangements.

FLIGHTS

All nonstop and direct air service is to Grand Cayman, with connecting flights to Cayman Brac and Little Cayman on a small propeller plane. Some flights only operate in high season. Cayman Airways offers nonstops from several destinations, including Chicago, Dallas, Miami, New York–JFK, and Tampa. All operate several times weekly except Miami, which is daily. American offers nonstop daily service from Miami and Charlotte. Delta flies weekly from Detroit, Minneapolis, and New York–JFK, and several times weekly from its Atlanta hub. JetBlue flies nonstop daily from JFK and seasonally from Boston. United flies weekly from Washington Dulles and Newark, and daily from Houston. Cayman Airways also flies to both Cayman Brac and Little Cayman. Canadian carrier WestJet flies nonstop three times weekly from Toronto. There's also interisland charter service on Island Air.

Airline Contacts American Airlines. ☎ *345/949–0666* ⊕ *www. aa.com.* **Cayman Airways.** ☎ *345/949–2311* ⊕ *www.caymanairways.com.* **Delta.** ☎ *345/945–8430* ⊕ *www.delta.com.* **Island Air.** ☎ *345/949–5252* ⊕ *www.islandair.ky.* **JetBlue.** ☎ *855/710–2951* ⊕ *www. jetblue.com.* **United.** ☎ *800/241–6522* ⊕ *www.united.com.* **WestJet.** ☎ *888/937–8538* ⊕ *www.westjet.com.*

▮ BIKE AND MOPED TRAVEL

When renting a motor scooter or bicycle, remember to drive on the left and wear sunblock and a helmet. Bicycles ($15 a day) and scooters ($50 a day) can be rented in George Town when cruise ships are in port. On Cayman Brac or Little Cayman your hotel can make arrangements for you (most offer complimentary bicycles for local sightseeing). There are two scooter companies on Little Cayman.

Rental Companies Island Scooter Rentals. ☎ *345/949–2046.* **Scoot Around Little Cayman.** ☎ *345/924–6229, 345/916–0656.* **Scooten! Scooters!** ☎ *345/916–4971* ⊕ *www. scootenscooters.com.*

▮ BUS TRAVEL

On Grand Cayman, bus service is efficient, inexpensive, and plentiful, running roughly every 15 minutes. Minivans marked "Omni Bus" are mostly independently operated (there are roughly 40 buses and 24 owners) and run from 6 am to 11 pm (until midnight Friday and Saturday) from West Bay to Rum Point and the East End; service on Sunday is limited. All routes branch from the George Town terminal adjacent to the library on Edward Street and are described in the phone book; color codes denote the nine routes. The one-way fare from George Town to West Bay via Seven Mile Beach is CI$2, to East End destinations CI$3, and from West Bay and northern Seven Mile Beach to East End CI$3.50. Some bus stops are well marked;

others are flexible. Respond to an approaching bus with a wave; then the driver toots his horn to acknowledge that he has seen you.

Bus Information Hotline. ☏ *345/945–5100* ⊕ *thebusschedule.com/EN/ky.*

▌ CAR TRAVEL

Driving is easy on Grand Cayman, albeit on the left. Most visitors, especially if they're staying along Seven Mile Beach, are content taking taxis or a one-day tour to see the sights rather than renting a car. Traffic on the road from Seven Mile Beach to George Town then onto Bodden Town in Grand Cayman is terrible, especially during the 7 to 9 am and 4:30 to 6:30 pm commuting periods, despite construction of two bypass roads. Fortunately, roads are generally well marked and well maintained. One major coastal highway circumnavigates most of the island (one shortcut bisects the extensive East Districts), though you can get lost in the tangle of side roads in primarily residential West Bay. Exploring Cayman Brac on a scooter is fun and straightforward. You won't really need a car on Little Cayman, though there are a limited number of jeeps for rent; bikes are the preferred mode of transport.

GASOLINE

In Grand Cayman, you can find gasoline stations in and around George Town, the airport, and Seven Mile Beach. Although times vary, most open daily with hours that extend into the evening; a few remain open 24 hours a day. There are two gasoline stations on Cayman Brac and one on Little Cayman. Prices are exorbitant, even compared to those in the United States and most of the Caribbean, especially on the Sister Islands.

PARKING

Park only in approved parking areas. Most hotels offer free parking. Many airport, Camana Bay, George Town, and Seven Mile Beach parking lots are free, but increasing development has prompted some major shopping centers to charge a fee if you park for more than 15 minutes (about $2.50 per hour); however, if you purchase something, parking should be validated and free. There is limited street parking, but watch for signs indicating private parking (in lots as well). Private enforcement companies are employed to discourage interlopers, placing a boot on the wheel and charging CI$75 for removal.

ROAD CONDITIONS

Grand Cayman has well-paved roads that follow the coastline. A network of main highways and bypasses facilitates traffic flow into and out of George Town. Small signs tacked to trees and poles at intersections point the way to most attractions, and local people are helpful if you get lost. Remote roads are in good repair, yet lighting can be poor at night—and night falls quickly at about 6 pm year-round.

Cayman Brac has one major road that skirts the coast, with a shortcut (Ashton Reid Drive) climbing the Bluff roughly bisecting the island. Little Cayman also provides a coastal route; unpaved sections in less-trammeled areas can become almost impassable after heavy rain. Other than that, goats, chickens, cattle, and the occasional iguana have the right of way.

ROADSIDE EMERGENCIES

Each car-rental agency has a different emergency-assistance provider. In the event of theft, accidents, or breakdowns, call your car-rental agency and follow instructions.

RULES OF THE ROAD

Be mindful of pedestrians and, in the countryside, occasional livestock walking on the road. When someone flashes headlights at you at an intersection, it means "after you." Be especially careful negotiating roundabouts (traffic circles). Observe the speed limit, which is conservative: 30 mph (50 kph) in the country, 20 mph (30 kph) in town. George Town actually has rush hours: 7 to 9 am and 4:30 to 6:30 pm. Park only in approved parking areas. Always wear your seat belts—it's the law!

CAR RENTAL

To rent a car in the Cayman Islands, you must have a valid driver's license and major credit card. Most agencies require renters to be between 21 and 70 years of age, though the minimum age may be 25. Those over 70 may need a certified doctor's note indicating a continuing ability to drive safely. A local driver's permit, which costs $20, is obtained through the rental agency. Several dozen agencies rent cars, 4WD vehicles, and SUVs; rates are expensive—ranging from $45 to $95 per day (or ranging from $250 to $600 or more per week) in high season, depending on the vehicle and whether it has air-conditioning. Many firms offer significant discounts in low season, as well as reduced three-day rates. The rental generally includes insurance, pickup and delivery service (or shuttle service to your hotel or the airport), maps, 24-hour emergency service, and unlimited mileage. Car seats are usually available upon request.

The major agencies have offices to the left as you depart from the airport terminal in Grand Cayman; the closest, Andy's, is to the right. All require that you walk outdoors for a hundred yards. Make sure your luggage is portable, because there's no shuttle; if there are two of you, one can watch the bags while the other gets the car. Many car-rental firms have free pickup and drop-off along Seven Mile Beach (or second branches) so you can rent just on the days you want to tour. Consider security when renting a jeep that cannot be locked. Midsize cars here often mean subcompact.

Grand Cayman Agencies Ace Hertz. ☎ *800/654–3131, 855/212–1713 toll-free, 345/943–4378* ⊕ *www.hertzcayman.com.* **Andy's Rent a Car.** ☎ *345/949–8111, 855/691–3991 toll-free* ⊕ *www.andys.ky.* **Avis.** ☎ *345/949–2468* ⊕ *www.aviscayman.com.* **Budget.** ☎ *345/949–5605* ⊕ *www.budgetcayman.com.* **Cayman Auto Rentals.** ✉ *N. Church St., George Town* ☎ *345/949–1013* ⊕ *www.caymanautorentals.com.ky.* **Dollar.** ☎ *345/949–4790* ⊕ *www.dollar.com.*

Economy. ☎ *345/949–9550* ⊕ *www. economycarrental.com.ky.* **Thrifty.** ☎ *345/949–6640, 800/367–2277* ⊕ *www.thrifty.com.*

Cayman Brac Agencies B&S Motor Ventures. ☎ *345/948–1646* ⊕ *www.bandsmv.com.* **CB Rent-a-Car.** ☎ *345/948–2424, 345/948–2424* ⊕ *www.cbrentacar.com.* **Four D's Car Rental.** ☎ *345/948–1599, 345/948–0459.*

Little Cayman Agencies Little Cayman Car Rental. ☎ *345/948–1000* ✉ *littlcay@candw.ky.*

CAR INSURANCE

If you own a car, your personal auto insurance may cover a rental to some degree, though not all policies protect you abroad; always read your policy's fine print. If you don't have auto insurance, consider buying the collision- or loss-damage waiver (CDW or LDW) from the car-rental company, which eliminates your liability for damage to the car.

Some credit cards offer CDW coverage, but it's usually supplemental to your own insurance and rarely covers SUVs, minivans, luxury models, and the like. If your coverage is secondary, you may still be liable for loss-of-use costs from the car-rental company. But no credit-card insurance is valid unless you use that card for *all* transactions, from reserving to paying the final bill. All companies exclude car rental in some countries, so be sure to find out about the destination to which you are traveling.

▌ TAXI TRAVEL

On Grand Cayman, taxis operate 24 hours a day; if you anticipate a late night, however, make pickup arrangements in advance. Call for a cab to be dispatched, as you generally cannot hail one on the street except occasionally in George Town. They carry up to three passengers for the same price. Fares aren't metered; the government sets rates, and they're not cheap, so ask ahead. The tariff increases with the number of riders and bags. To travel in style by limo, you can call A.A. Transportation or Grand Limousine Services. Drivers are courteous and knowledgeable; most will narrate a tour at an hourly rate of about $25 for up to three people. Be sure to settle the price before you start off and agree on whether it's quoted in U.S. or Cayman dollars.

Taxis are scarcer on the Sister Islands; rates are also fixed and fairly prohibitive. Your hotel will provide recommended drivers.

Taxi Companies A.A. Transportation Services. ☎ *345/926–8294* ⊕ *www.aatransportation.weebly.com.* **Charlie's Super Cab.** ☎ *345/926–4748, 345/926–6590* ⊕ *www. charliescabs.net.* **Grand Limousine Services.** ☎ *345/916–7772* ⊕ *www. limo.ky.*

ESSENTIALS

■ ACCOMMODATIONS

Grand Cayman offers a wide range of lodgings in all price categories (though it ranks as one of the more expensive Caribbean destinations). You'll find luxury resorts, hotels both large and intimate, fully equipped condos, stylish individual villas, B&Bs, and more affordable locally run guesthouses. Quality, professionalism, high-tech conveniences, and service all rank among the region's best. With a few notable exceptions, condo resorts rule Seven Mile Beach (some hotels lie across the coastal "highway"). These are particularly attractive family options, as they include kitchen facilities. Cayman Brac and Little Cayman accommodations emphasize function above glitz and glamour (though most lack neither character nor characters), befitting the Sister Islands' status as top-notch scuba-diving destinations. Both have villas, condo resorts, and small hotels that often run on an all-inclusive or meal-plan basis and simple, family-run inns.

■ COMMUNICATIONS

INTERNET

In Grand Cayman most hotels and resorts provide Internet access—either free or for a small fee—for their guests; wireless is increasingly prevalent, including at the airport in Grand Cayman. You'll also find Internet cafés in George Town. Rates range from $2.50 for 15 minutes to $10 per hour. Sev-

eral restaurants also advertise free Wi-Fi hotspots. Although there are no cybercafés on the Sister Islands, most of the small hotels have high-speed access in rooms and/or public spaces. Those lacking Wi-Fi or high-speed Internet connections in rooms usually have a public computer or permit use of the office facilities. A few individual villas offer Wi-Fi.

PHONES

The area code for the Cayman Islands is 345.

CALLING WITHIN THE CAYMAN ISLANDS

In the Cayman Islands local calls are free from private phones; some hotels charge a small fee. For directory assistance, dial 411; international directory assistance is 010. Calls from pay phones cost CI¢25 for five minutes. Prepaid phone cards, which can be used throughout Cayman and other Caribbean islands, are sold at shops, attractions, transportation centers, and other convenient outlets.

CALLING OUTSIDE THE CAYMAN ISLANDS

From the Cayman Islands, direct dialing to the United States and other countries is efficient and reasonable, but always check with your hotel to see if a surcharge is added. Some toll-free numbers cannot be accessed, especially on the Sister Islands. To charge your overseas call on a major credit card or

U.S. calling card without incurring a surcharge, dial 800/225–5872 (1–800/CALL–USA) from any phone.

The country code for the United States is 1.

Information **AT&T.** ☏ 800/872–2881. **FLOW.** ☏ 345/949–7800 in Grand Cayman.

CALLING CARDS

LIME phone cards, which can be used for both local and international calls, are available for purchase in various denominations at many retail outlets, including supermarkets and gas stations. They can be used from any touchtone telephone (including pay and cell phones) in the Cayman Islands. The rates on-island are competitive with those of online servers and more reliable.

MOBILE PHONES

If you're bringing your own mobile phone and it's compatible with 850/1900 Mhz GSM network or TDMA digital network, you should be able to make and receive calls during your stay, especially from Grand Cayman. Be sure, however, to check with your home provider that you have roaming service enabled, and note that charges can be astronomical depending on your calling plan. Renting a cell phone if you're planning an extended vacation or expect to make a lot of local calls may be a less expensive alternative than using your own. Mobile-phone rental is available from FLOW (formerly Cable & Wireless) and Digicel; you can stay connected for as little as CI$5 per day plus the cost of a calling card (denominations range from CI$10 to CI$100). International per-minute rates usually range from CI¢35 to CI¢60. You can rent phones for use on-island from either LIME or Digicel.

Mobile Phone Companies **Digicel.** ✉ Leeward One, Regatta Office Park, 1158A West Bay Rd., Seven Mile Beach ☏ 345/623–3445 ⊕ www.digicelgroup.com. **FLOW.** ✉ Anderson Square Bldg., Shedden Rd., George Town ☏ 345/949–7800 ⊕ www.discoverflow.ky ✉ Galleria Plaza, West Bay Rd., Seven Mile Beach ⊕ www.discoverflow.ky.

▌ CUSTOMS AND DUTIES

Travelers to the Cayman Islands should not note any problems at customs. It typically takes fewer than 10 minutes to clear, even during large on-island events. Items to declare upon arrival include any large video or camera equipment so that Immigration does not assume the traveler may have work permits or is trying to film/shoot photos professionally without prior consent. Some perishable foodstuffs and plants may require permits. Regulations regarding pets are strict and complex. In brief, they must be at least 10 months old; you must fill out an Import Permit application and include a medical certificate, rabies lab report, and fee, and implant a microchip or tattoo the animal for identification purposes. For all information and appropriate downloadable forms, consult the Cayman Islands Customs website.

Contacts **Cayman Islands Customs.** ☎ 345/949–4579 ⊕ customs. gov.ky.

EATING OUT

Obviously seafood reigns supreme in the Cayman Islands, where it's served everywhere from tiny family-run shanties to decadently decorated bistros. But befitting Grand Cayman's reputation as a sophisticated, multinational destination (with residents from 120 countries at last count), you can find a smorgasbord of savory options from terrific Tex-Mex to Thai to Italian. Menus could highlight by-the-book bouillabaisse or barbecue, kebabs or cannelloni, ceviche or sushi. This is one destination where larger resorts generally have excellent restaurants. Two must-try local delicacies are conch, particularly fritters and chowder, and turtle (protected but farmed); the latter is stewed or served like a steak. Many restaurants offer kids' menus, and vegetarians should find acceptable options.

MEALS AND MEALTIMES

Most restaurants serve breakfast from 7 to 10 am, lunch from noon to 3 pm, and dinner from 6 to 11 pm. But these hours can vary widely, especially at remote resorts on Grand Cayman's East End and West Bay, as well as on the Sister Islands, which have few independent eateries. Every strip mall along Grand Cayman's Seven Mile Beach has at least one restaurant open late (often doubling as a lounge or nightclub); many beachfront bars also offer late dining, especially on weekends. Restaurants are likeliest to shutter on Sunday, especially in the less-trafficked areas. Since most grocery stores also close Sunday, prepare for contingencies, especially if you're staying at an individual villa or condo. If you arrive on Saturday, when most villa and condo rentals begin, make sure you do your grocery shopping that afternoon.

PAYING

Major credit cards are widely accepted, even on the Sister Islands, though some smaller local establishments only accept cash.

RESERVATIONS AND DRESS

Grand Cayman is both cosmopolitan and conservative, so scantily clad diners are frowned upon or downright refused seating. Many tonier establishments require long pants and collared shirts for gentlemen in the evening (lunch is generally more casual). Footwear and something to cover bathing suits (a sarong or sundress for women, T-shirt and shorts for men) are required save at some beachfront bars. The Sister Islands are far more casual. Reservations are strongly recommended for dinner at most restaurants throughout the islands.

We mention dress only when men are required to wear a jacket or a jacket and tie.

BEER, WINE, AND SPIRITS

Beer, wine, and spirits are readily available at most restaurants. Some pricier restaurants take great pride in their wine lists. Aficionados of local products may want to try the refreshing Caybrew beers (the nutty, smoky dark amber pairs well with many foods), Seven Fathoms rum, and Tortuga rum (the 12-year-old is a marvelous after-dinner sipper in place of Cognac or single-malt Scotch).

▌ EMERGENCIES

Emergency Services Ambulance. ☎ 911. **Fire.** ☎ 911. **Police.** ☎ 911.

Foreign Consulates U.S. Consular Agency. ✉ 202B Smith Road Cayman Centre, 150 Smith Rd., George Town ☎ 345/945–8173 ⌂ caymanacs@state.gov.

Hospitals The Brac Clinic. ✉ Tibbetts Sq., West End ☎ 345/949–1777 ⊕ www.bracmed.com. **Cayman Clinic.** ☎ 345/949–4234. **Faith Hospital.** ✉ Dennis Foster Rd., Stake Bay ☎ 345/948–2243. **George Town Hospital.** ✉ 1 Hospital Rd., George Town ☎ 345/949–8600. **Health City Cayman.** ✉ 1283 Sea View Rd., East End ☎ 345/640–4040 ⊕ www.healthcitycaymanislands.com.

TrinCay Medical Centre. ✉ 55 Market St., Suite 1204, Camana Bay ☎ 345/943–4633 ⊕ www.trincay.ky.

Pharmacies Cayman Drug. ✉ Kirk Freeport Centre, George Town ☎ 345/949–2597. **Foster's Pharmacy.** ✉ Foster's Food Fair, Airport Rd., George Town ☎ 345/949–0505 ⊕ www.fosters-iga.com. **Health Care Pharmacy.** ✉ Governor's Square, Seven Mile Beach ☎ 345/949–8900 ⊕ www.healthcarepharmacy.ky. **Kirk Pharmacy.** ✉ Kirk Supermarket, Eastern Ave., George Town ☎ 345/949–7180 ⊕ www.kirkmarket.ky.

Diving Emergencies Cayman Hyperbaric. ✉ 95 Hospital Rd., George Town ☎ 345/949–2989, 345/916–1957.

▌ HEALTH

Health concerns are minimal in the Cayman Islands, and Grand Cayman offers some of the Caribbean's finest medical facilities. Though there have been isolated cases of dengue fever (one or two annually, contracted elsewhere), the last on-island outbreak was in 2005. The CDC does recommend hepatitis A and typhoid vaccinations to be on the safe side. Airlift to Miami for serious emergencies is available. Physicians are highly qualified and speak English. Be sure to pack prescription medications; consider wearing a MedicAlert ID tag if you suffer from such chronic conditions as diabetes, epilepsy, or heart disease. Though many hospitals offer reciprocity with U.S. insurers, you can also purchase medical-only insurance. Tap water is perfectly safe to drink throughout all three islands. Be sure to wash fruit thoroughly or, better yet, peel it before eating. The subtropic sun can be fierce, especially at midday. Be sure to wear sunglasses and a hat, and use high-SPF sunscreen (most U.S. brands are available). Beware of dehydration and heat stroke; take it easy the first couple of days. Insects can be a real nuisance during the wet season (July–November); bring along repellent to ward off mosquitoes and sand flies. Shops also stock numerous name brands.

MEDICAL INSURANCE AND ASSISTANCE

Consider buying trip insurance with medical-only coverage. Neither Medicare nor some private insurers cover medical expenses anywhere outside the United

States. Medical-only policies typically reimburse you for medical care (excluding that related to pre-existing conditions) and hospitalization abroad and provide for evacuation. You still have to pay the bills and await reimbursement from the insurer, though.

Another option is to sign up with a medical-evacuation assistance company. A membership in one of these companies gets you doctor referrals, emergency evacuation or repatriation, 24-hour hotlines for medical consultation, and other assistance. International SOS Assistance Emergency and AirMed International provide evacuation services and medical referrals. MedjetAssist offers medical evacuation.

Medical Assistance Companies **AirMed International.** ☎ *800/356–2161* ⊕ *www.airmed.com.* **International SOS Assistance Emergency.** ⊕ *www.internationalsos.com.* **MedjetAssist.** ☎ *800/527–7478* ⊕ *www.medjetassist.com.*

Health Information **National Centers for Disease Control & Prevention** (*CDC*). ☎ *877/394–8747 international travelers' health line* ⊕ *www.cdc.gov/travel.* **World Health Organization** (*WHO*). ⊕ *www.who.int.*

Medical-Only Insurers **International Medical Group.** ☎ *800/628–4664* ⊕ *www.imglobal.com.* **Wallach and Company.** ☎ *800/237–6615, 540/687–3166, 800/237–6615 toll-free* ⊕ *www.wallach.com.*

▌ **HOURS OF OPERATION**

Banks in the Cayman Islands are generally open weekdays from 9 to 3. Post offices are open weekdays from 8:30 to 4 and Saturday from 9 to 1. Shops are usually open weekdays from 9 to 5; in outer shopping plazas they are open from 10 to 5. Shops are usually closed Sunday except in hotels or when cruise ships are visiting. Pharmacy hours vary, most opening between 7 and 9 am, closing between 6 and 10 pm; most also close Sunday.

HOLIDAYS

In the Cayman Islands public holidays include New Year's Day, Ash Wednesday (46 days before Easter), Good Friday (Friday before Easter), Easter Sunday (usually March or April), Discovery Day (May 19), Queen's Birthday (June 16), Constitution Day (July 7), Remembrance Day (November 17), Christmas, and Boxing Day (December 26). The last refers to boxing extra presents for charity, not prizefighting!

▌ **MAIL**

Sending a postcard to the United States, Canada, other parts of the Caribbean, or Central America costs CI25¢. An airmail letter is CI75¢ per half ounce. To Europe and South America, rates are CI25¢ for a postcard and CI80¢ per half ounce for airmail letters. When addressing letters to the Cayman Islands, be sure to include the new postal codes that have been introduced. You can find them at ⊕ *www.caymanpost.gov.ky* or on leaflets at any of the islands' post offices. The main post office lies at the intersection of Edward Street and Cardinal Avenue in downtown George Town. There is no home delivery; instead, all mail is delivered to numbered post-office boxes. For faster and reliable service to the United States, Federal Express, UPS, and DHL all have locations in the downtown area. Airmail can take two weeks to be delivered to farther-flung areas, including Australia and New Zealand.

▌MONEY

You should not need to change money in Grand Cayman, because U.S. dollars are readily accepted, though you may get some change in Cayman dollars. ATMs accepting MasterCard and Visa with Cirrus affiliation are readily available in George Town; you usually have the option of U.S. or Cayman dollars. The Cayman dollar is pegged to the U.S. dollar at the rate of approximately CI$1 to $1.25, and divided into a hundred cents, with coins of 1¢, 5¢, 10¢, and 25¢ and notes of $1, $5, $10, $25, $50, and $100. There's no $20 bill. Traveler's checks and major credit cards are widely accepted. Be sure you know which currency is being quoted when making a purchase.

CREDIT CARDS

It's a good idea to inform your credit-card company before you travel. Record all your credit-card numbers—as well as the phone numbers to call if your cards are lost or stolen—in a safe place, so you're prepared should something go wrong. Both MasterCard and Visa have general numbers you can call (collect if you're abroad) if your card is lost, but you're better off calling the number of your issuing bank, since MasterCard and Visa usually just transfer you to your bank; your bank's number is usually printed on your card.

If you plan to use your credit card for cash advances, you'll need to apply for a PIN at least two weeks before your trip. Although it's usually cheaper (and safer) to use a credit card abroad for large purchases (so you can cancel payments or be reimbursed if there's a problem), note that some credit-card companies *and* the banks that issue them add substantial percentages to all foreign transactions, whether they're in a foreign currency or not. Check on these fees before leaving home, so there won't be any surprises when you get the bill.

▌PASSPORTS AND VISAS

All visitors to the Cayman Islands must have a valid passport and a return or ongoing ticket to enter the Cayman Islands. A birth certificate and photo ID are *not* sufficient proof of citizenship.

▌SAFETY

Though crime isn't a major problem in the Cayman Islands, take normal precautions. Lock your room, and don't leave valuables—particularly passports, tickets, and wallets—in plain sight or unattended on the beach. Use your hotel safe. Don't carry too much money or flaunt expensive jewelry on the street. For personal safety, avoid walking on the beach or on unlighted streets at night. Lock your rental car, and don't pick up hitchhikers. Using or trafficking in illegal drugs is strictly prohibited in the Cayman Islands. Any offense is punishable by a hefty fine, imprisonment, or both.

▌ TAXES AND SERVICE CHARGES

At the airport, each adult passenger leaving Grand Cayman must pay a departure tax of $25 (CI$20), payable in either Caymanian or U.S. currency. It may be included in cruise packages as a component of port charges; it's usually added to airfare—check with your carrier—but if not, must be paid in cash by each traveler prior to entering the secure area of the airport.

A 10% government tax is added to all hotel bills. A 10% service charge is often added to hotel bills and restaurant checks in lieu of a tip. There is no VAT or comparable tariff on goods and services.

▌ TIME

U.S. eastern standard time (EST), five hours behind Greenwich mean time (GMT–0500), is in effect year-round on all three islands; daylight saving time is not observed.

▌ TIPPING

At large hotels a service charge is generally included and can be anywhere from 6% to 10%; smaller establishments and some villas and condos leave tipping up to you. Although tipping is customary at restaurants, note that some automatically include 10%–15% on the bill—so check the tab carefully. At your discretion, tip another 5% or more to recognize extraordinary service. Taxi drivers expect a 10%–15% tip. Bellmen and porters expect $1 per bag, more in luxury hotels (especially if you bring lots of luggage). Tip the concierge (if your resort has one) anywhere from $10 to $100, depending on services rendered and length of stay. Tips are not expected simply for handing out maps and making the occasional dinner reservation. Spa personnel should receive 15%–20% of the treatment price (but verify that a service fee wasn't already added).

▌ TOURS

GUIDED TOURS

A sightseeing tour is a good way to get your bearings and to experience Caymanian culture. Taxi drivers will give you a personalized tour of Grand Cayman for about $25 per hour for up to three people. Or you can choose a fascinating helicopter ride, a horseback or mountain-bike journey, a 4x4 safari expedition, or a full-day bus excursion. The prices vary according to the mode of travel and the number and kind of attractions included. Ask your hotel to help you make arrangements.

Costs and itineraries for island tours are about the same regardless of the tour operator. Half-day tours average $40–$50 a person and generally include a visit to Hell and the Turtle Centre at Boatswain's Beach in West Bay, as well as shopping downtown. Full-day tours ($60–

$80 per person) add lunch, a visit to Bodden Town (the first settlement), and the East End, where you stop at the Queen Elizabeth II Botanic Park, blowholes (if the waves are high) on the ironshore, and the site of the wreck of the *Ten Sails* (not the wreck itself—just the site). The pirate graves in Bodden Town were destroyed during Hurricane Ivan, and the blowholes were partially filled. As you can tell, land tours here are low-key. Children under 12 often receive discounts.

A.A. Transportation Services offers taxis and tour buses. Ask for Burton Ebanks. B.A. McCurley, owner of McCurley Tours, is a free-spirited, freewheeling midwesterner who's lived in Cayman for 24 years and knows everything and everyone on the East End. Not only is she encyclopedic and flexible, she also offers car rentals and transfers for travelers staying on the East End; don't be surprised if she tells you what to order at lunch, especially if it's off the menu. The guides at Webster's are friendly, local, and well-versed in island info and lore; they're also a good resource for airport transfers.

Majestic Tours caters mostly to cruise-ship and incentive groups but also offers similar options to individuals and can customize tours; it's particularly good for West Bay, including the Turtle Centre and Hell.

Tropicana Tours offers several excellent Cayman highlights itineraries on its larger buses, including Stingray City stops, as well as reef-runner adventures across the North Sound through the mangrove swamps.

Your hotel or villa agent can recommend and organize drivers for tours of the Sister Islands.

Contacts A.A. Transportation Services. ☎ 345/949–6598, 345/926–8294, 345/949–7222 ⊕ www.aatransportation.weebly.com. **Majestic Tours.** ☎ 345/949–7773 ⊕ www.majestictours.ky. **McCurley Tours.** ☎ 345/947–9626, 345/916–0925 ✉ mccurley@cwhiptop.com. **Tropicana Tours.** ☎ 345/949–0944 ⊕ www.tropicana-tours.com. **Webster's Tours.** ☎ 345/945–1433 ⊕ www.websters.ky.

SPECIAL-INTEREST TOURS
Cayman Custom Cycles' Harley Davidson tours allow you to go hog wild, wind in your face, exploring the East End. Tours run $200–$275 (the full-day option includes lunch). Additional passengers can hitch a ride for $50.

Cayman Island Helicopters offers exhilarating eagle-eye views on three itineraries: $79 for a flyover of Seven Mile Beach; $145 for a trip adding Stingray City; and $355 for a thrillingly panoramic island-wide aerial tour (discounts are available if you book via the company's website, and shuttle service is free). Though the island is flat and mostly arid, the sight of waters rippling from turquoise to tourmaline is exciting enough.

Cayman Safari's 4WD tours hit the usual sights but emphasize interaction with locals, so you learn about craft traditions, folklore, and herbal medicines.

Contacts **Cayman Custom Cycles Harley Davidson Tours.** ☎ *345/945–7433, 345/916–0088* ⊕ *www.caymancustomcycles.com.* **Cayman Island Helicopters.** ☎ *345/943–4354, 345/926–6967* ⊕ *www.caymanislandshelicopters. com.* **Cayman Safari.** ☎ *345/925– 3002* ⊕ *www.caymansafari.com.*

▮ TRIP INSURANCE

Comprehensive trip insurance is valuable if you're booking a very expensive or complicated trip (particularly to an isolated region) or if you're booking far in advance. Comprehensive policies typically cover trip cancellation and interruption, letting you cancel or cut your trip short because of illness or, in some cases, acts of terrorism in your destination. Such policies might also cover evacuation and medical care. (For trips abroad you should have at least medical-only coverage.) Some also cover you for trip delays because of bad weather or mechanical problems as well as for lost or delayed luggage.

Another type of coverage to consider is financial default—that is, when your trip is disrupted because a tour operator, airline, or cruise line goes out of business. Generally you must buy this when you book your trip or shortly thereafter, and it's available to you only if your operator isn't on a list of excluded companies.

Insurance Comparison Sites **Insure My Trip.** ☎ *800/487–4722* ⊕ *www.insuremytrip.com.* **Square Mouth.** ☎ *800/240–0369* ⊕ *www. squaremouth.com.*

Travel Insurers **AIG Travel Guard.** ☎ *800/826–4919* ⊕ *www. travelguard.com.* **Allianz Global Assistance.** ☎ *800/284–8300* ⊕ *www.allianztravelinsurance. com.* **CSA Travel Protection.** ☎ *800/243–4135* ⊕ *www.csatravel-protection.com.* **Travelex Insurance.** ☎ *800/228–9792* ⊕ *www.travelex-insurance.com.* **Travel Insured International.** ☎ *800/243–3174* ⊕ *www. travelinsured.com.*

▮ VISITOR INFORMATION

The Cayman Islands has tourist offices in the United States, where you can get brochures and maps in advance of your trip. There are also tourism offices on the islands for on-site help.

Cayman Islands Department of Tourism. ☎ *212/889–9009 in New York City, 877/422–9626 in U.S., 345/949–0623 in Caymans* ⊕ *www.caymanislands.ky.*

Department of Tourism. ✉ *Regatta Office Park Windward 3, West Bay Rd., Seven Mile Beach* ☎ *345/949– 0623* ⊕ *caymanislands.ky* ✉ *West End Rd., North Side* ☎ *345/948– 1649* ✉ *Owen Roberts Airport* ☎ *345/949–3603.*

ONLINE RESOURCES

Caymanian Compass. *Caymanian Compass, the online version of the national newspaper, offers news, occasionally provocative commentary, event listings, weather reports, currency converter, photo galleries, interactive map, and the CaymanEye live Webcam.* ⊕ *www. compasscayman.com.*

Cayman Islands Destination Magazine. *Cayman Islands Destination Magazine* provides information on everything from airlines to accommodations, restaurants to real estate, with useful links. ⊕ *www.destination.ky.*

Cayman Islands Vacations and Business Directory. *Cayman Islands Vacations and Business Directory,* funded by private-sector businesses, functions as a de facto Chamber of Commerce adjunct, with extensive transportation, lodging, dining, recreational, bar-hopping, and shopping write-ups, as well as information on everything from marine conservation to culture, weather to weddings. ⊕ *www.caymanchamber.ky.*

Cayman News Service Online. Cayman News Service Online provides all the daily local news that's fit to cyberprint. ⊕ *www.caymannewsservice.com.*

Cayman Restaurant Guide. Cayman Restaurant Guide is a fairly comprehensive listing of eateries with sample menus, maps, reviews, even recipes. ⊕ *www.caymanrestaurants.com.*

Good Taste. Good Taste bills itself as "Cayman's definitive dining and entertainment guide," dishing out menus for dozens of restaurants, alongside articles on local cuisine and charts detailing which eateries offer children's portions, alfresco dining, water views, and more. ⊕ *www.caymangoodtaste.com.*

It's Yours to Explore. It's Yours to Explore is a useful, privately run adjunct to the official Sister Islands websites, offering lots of local news and gossip, photos, and often faster updates. ⊕ *www.itsyourstoexplore.com.*

Key to Cayman. Key to Cayman is the online version of a thick, stylish quarterly with particular focus on shopping, real estate, heritage, attractions, and crafts. ⊕ *www.keytocayman.com.*

National Trust for the Cayman Islands. National Trust for the Cayman Islands is an admirable nonprofit institution dedicated to preserving the cultural, historic, and environmental heritage of the Cayman Islands. Its informative website includes information on programs, maps, events, and more. ⊕ *www.nationaltrust.org.ky.*

Nature Cayman. Nature Cayman details the sister islands' rich flora and fauna on land and underwater, along with detailed coverage of Cayman Brac and Little Cayman history and culture. ⊕ *www.naturecayman.com.*

Sister Islands Tourism Association. Sister Islands Tourism Association is the website of a business group that publicizes its member establishments on Cayman Brac and Little Cayman. ⊕ *www.sita.ky.*

Tourism Attraction Board. Tourism Attraction Board runs several of Grand Cayman's leading attractions and events, including Pedro St. James historical site, Queen Elizabeth II Botanic Park, and November's annual Pirates Week Festival. ⊕ *www.tab.ky.*

▮ WEDDINGS

Getting married in the Cayman Islands is a breeze, and each year many couples tie the knot here. Most choose to say their vows on lovely Seven Mile Beach, with the sun setting into the azure sea as their picture-perfect backdrop. Underwater weddings in full scuba gear with schools of fish as impromptu witnesses are also possible (kissing with mask on optional). Cathy Church can photograph your underwater wedding (⇨ *see Shopping in Chapter 2*). You can literally leave things up in the air, getting hitched while hovering in a helicopter. A traditional church wedding can even be arranged, after which you trot away to your life together in a horse-drawn carriage.

Documentation can be prepared ahead of time or in one day while on the island. There's no on-island waiting period. In addition to the application, you need proof of identity and age (those under 18 must provide parental consent), such as an original or certified birth certificate or passport; a Cayman Islands international embarkation/disembarkation card; and certified or original copies of divorce decrees/death certificates if you have been married before. You must list a marriage officer on the application, and you need at least two witnesses; if you haven't come with friends or family, the marriage officer can help you with that, too. A marriage license costs CI$200 (US$250).

The best way to plan your wedding in the Cayman Islands is to contact a wedding coordinator (resorts such as the Wyndham Reef, Westin Grand Cayman, Kimpton Seafire, and Ritz-Carlton have one on staff), who will offer a wide variety of packages to suit every taste and budget. All the logistics and legalities will be properly handled, giving you time to relax and enjoy the wedding of your dreams. The Cayman Islands Department of Tourism also keeps a list of recommended independent wedding coordinators. Or you can order the brochure "Getting Married in the Cayman Islands" from Government Information Services. You can choose from many different styles of services or rewrite one as you wish.

Information Deputy Chief Secretary. ✉ *Government Administration Bldg., 3rd fl., George Town* ☎ *345/949–7900, 345/914–2222.* **District Commissioner's Office.** ✉ *District Administration Bldg., Stake Bay* ☎ *345/948–2222, 345/948–2506.* **Government Information Services.** ✉ *Cricket Sq., George Town* ☎ *345/949–8092.*

INDEX

PHOTO CREDITS

Front cover: Holger Leue/Getty Images/Lonely Planet Images[Description: Stingray City, Grand Cayman, Cayman Islands, Caribbean]. 1, SuperStock/age fotostock. 2, Stuart Pearce / age fotostock. 3 (top), Burrard-Lucas Photography/ Cayman Islands Department of Tourism. 3 (bottom), Mark Narsanski/Cayman Islands Department of Tourism. 4 (top left), Allister Clark/iStockphoto. 4 (top right), Pirates Point Resort. 4 (bottom), J & C Sohns / age fotostock. 5, Deep Blue/ Cayman Islands Department of Tourism. 6, Stephen Frink Collection / Alamy. 7 (top left), Zach Stovall/Bonnier Corporation. 7 (top right), Martyn Poynor. 7 (bottom), RENAULT Philippe / age fotostock. 8 (top left), Rohit Seth/Shutterstock. 8 (top right), Shimon & Tammer. 8 (bottom), Lawson Wood / age fotostock. 11, FLPA/age fotostock. **Chapter 1: Experience Cayman Islands:** 12-13, Don McDougall/Cayman Islands Department of Tourism. **Chapter 2: Exploring Grand Cayman:** 25, Johney13 | Dreamstime.com. 28, allyclark /istock. 32, Cayman Islands Department of Tourism. 36, SSImages Collection/iStockphoto. 38, Cayman Islands Department of Tourism. 40, Cayman Islands Department of Tourism. 48-49, Cayman Islands Department of Tourism. **Chapter 3: Where to Eat in Grand Cayman:** 55, Ortanique. 64, Mark Wieland. **Chapter 4: Where to Stay in Grand Cayman:** 75, Westin Hotels & Resorts. 77, aceshot1/Shutterstock. 80, Caribbean Club. 82-83, PixAchi/Shutterstock. 84, The Ritz-Carlton, Grand Cayman. 88, Dan McDougall/Cayman Islands Department of Tourism. 90, Courtney Platt. 92, Dan McDougall/Cayman Islands Department of Tourism. 93, Robert Smith/age fotostock. **Chapter 5: Grand Cayman Nightlife and the Arts:** 95, Mike Hoffman/Lone Star. 101, MCHart/Flickr. 102, Danita Delimont/ Alamy. **Chapter 6: Grand Cayman Sports and Outdoor Activities:** 109, Kevin Panizza/iStockphoto. 112-113, Jan Greune/age fotostock. 120, Peter Heiss/ iStockphoto. 122, Corbis. 129 and 132-133, Cayman Islands Department of Tourism. 136, Ronald J. Manera/iStockphoto. **Chapter 7: Cayman Brac:** 139, James Tibbetts/Cayman Islands Department of Tourism. 148, J & C Sohns/age fotostock. 151, Jan Greune/age fotostock. 154-155, RENAULT Philippe/age fotostock. 156, Kevin Panizza/iStockphoto. 162-163, Greg Johnston/age fotostock. **Chapter 8: Little Cayman:** 167, James Tibbetts/Cayman Islands Department of Tourism. 176, Dan McDougall/Cayman Islands Department of Tourism. 178, Cayman Islands Department of Tourism. 180-181, RENAULT Philippe/age fotostock. 182, Chris A. Crumley/Alamy. **Spine:** Amanda Nicholls/Shutterstock. **About Our Writers:** All photos are courtesy of the writers.

Fodor's InFocus CAYMAN ISLANDS

Editorial: Douglas Stallings, *Editorial Director*; Margaret Kelly, Jacinta O'Halloran, *Senior Editors*; Kayla Becker, Alexis Kelly, Amanda Sadlowski, *Editors*; Teddy Minford, *Content Editor*; Rachael Roth, *Content Manager*

Design: Tina Malaney, *Design and Production Director*; Jessica Gonzalez, *Production Designer*

Photography: Jennifer Arnow, *Senior Photo Editor*

Maps: Rebecca Baer, *Senior Map Editor*; David Lindroth, Mark Stroud (Moon Street Cartography), *Cartographers*

Production: Jennifer DePrima, *Editorial Production Manager*; Carrie Parker, *Senior Production Editor*; Elyse Rozelle, *Production Editor*

Business & Operations: Chuck Hoover, *Chief Marketing Officer*; Joy Lai, *Vice President and General Manager*; Stephen Horowitz, *Director of Business Development and Revenue Operations*; Tara McCrillis, *Director of Publishing Operations*; Eliza D. Aceves, *Content Operations Manager and Strategist*

Public Relations and Marketing: Joe Ewaskiw, *Manager*; Esther Su, *Marketing Manager*

Writer: Jordan Simon

Editor: Rachael Roth

Production Editor: Carrie Parker

5th Edition

ISBN 978-1-64097-042-7

ISSN 1941–0220

SPECIAL SALES

This book is available at special discounts for bulk purchases for sales promotions or premiums. For more information, e-mail SpecialMarkets@fodors.com.

PRINTED IN THE UNITED STATES OF AMERICA

10 9 8 7 6 5 4 3 2 1

ABOUT OUR WRITER

Jordan Simon worked in various aspects of the entertainment industry, from actor to director, before defecting to journalism. He's served as editor of *Caribbean Living* and founding co-editor-in-chief of *Swanky Retreats*; food and/or wine editor for *Atlanta Homes & Lifestyles, Hamptons, Second Home, Snow Country,* and *Ski Impact*; contributing editor for *AOL Travel, Nikki Style, TAXI, I-MI,* and *Shermans Travel.* He oversaw development of *Wine Country International* as founding editor-in-chief. He's beachcombed for many magazines and websites, including *Caribbean Travel & Life, Condé Nast Traveler, Town & Country, Modern Bride, Diversion,* ShermansTravel.com, Jetsetter.com, *Cooking Light, Interval, Art & Antiques, USAir Magazine, TravelAge,* and *American Way.*

He's written several guidebooks, including the original editions of *Fodor's Colorado* and *Fodor's Branson: The Official Travel & Souvenir Guide.* He co-wrote *The Celestial Seasonings Cookbook: Cooking with Tea* with Mo and Jennifer Siegel; *Astronumerology: Your Key to Empowerment Using Stars & Numbers* with Pam Bell; and *Edge Atlanta* with Jeff Clark, et al.

EUGENE FODOR

Hungarian-born Eugene Fodor (1905–91) began his travel career as an interpreter on a French cruise ship. The experience inspired him to write *On the Continent* (1936), the first guidebook to receive annual updates and discuss a country's way of life as well as its sights. Fodor later joined the U.S. Army and worked for the OSS in World War II. After the war, he kept up his intelligence work while expanding his guidebook series. During the Cold War, many guides were written by fellow agents who understood the value of insider information. Today's guides continue Fodor's legacy by providing travelers with timely coverage, insider tips, and cultural context.